1500
DAYS OF WHOLESOME
CANNED RECIPES

AMISH
CANNING &
PRESERVING
COOKBOOK

THE COMPLETE WATERBATH RECIPES ON HOW TO MAKE DELICIOUS AND SIMPLE HOMEMADE SOUPS, SAUCES, PICKLES, AND MORE IN A JAR.

DR. GEORGINA TRACY

Amish Canning & Preserving Cookbook

THE COMPLETE WATERBATH RECIPES ON HOW TO MAKE DELICIOUS AND SIMPLE HOMEMADE SOUPS, SAUCES, PICKLES, AND MORE IN A JAR.

DR. GEORGINA TRACY & ELI YODER

Table of Contents

INTRODUCTION

As a doctor, I have always been fascinated by the healing powers of nature. And as someone who grew up in the heart of Pennsylvania, I have always been surrounded by the Amish community and their simple way of life. So when I found myself at a crossroads in my career, unsure of the path forward, it was only natural that I turned to the wisdom of the Amish for guidance.

That's when I reached out to my childhood friend, Eli Yoder, an Amish farmer whom I had known since I was a little girl. We had lost touch over the years, but I knew that Eli had inherited his family's farm and was still living the traditional Amish lifestyle. I was curious to see how his community had been impacted by modern medicine, and if there was anything I could learn from their approach to health and healing.

To my surprise, Eli was eager to reconnect and even more eager to share his knowledge with me. He invited me to spend a week on his farm, where he showed me the basics of canning and preserving foods, as well as the many medicinal plants and herbs that grew in the surrounding fields and forests.

It was a revelation. As a doctor, I had always believed that medicine was something that could only be obtained through a prescription, but here I was, learning how to make healing salves and tinctures from the plants that grew all around us. And as we worked side by side in his kitchen, canning jars of fresh produce and preserving them for the winter months ahead, I realized that the act of preserving food was itself a form of healing.

That's when the idea for this book began to take shape. Eli and I realized that we had stumbled upon something special, a way of life that combined the healing powers of nature with the practical skills of the Amish community. We wanted to share our knowledge with others, to show how simple it can be to preserve food and maintain good health, even in our fast-paced, modern world.

As we worked on this book, Eli and I poured our hearts and souls into every page. For me, it was a chance to reconnect with my roots and rediscover the simple pleasures of life. For Eli, it was an opportunity to share his community's traditions and teach others the skills he had learned from his ancestors.

We spent countless hours in the kitchen, testing recipes and perfecting techniques. We scoured the fields and forests for medicinal herbs and plants, carefully selecting the ones that held the most healing properties. And as we worked, we shared stories and memories, reminiscing about the past and dreaming of the future.

Through it all, we never lost sight of our goal. We wanted to create a book that would inspire others to live healthier, more sustainable lives. We wanted to show that preserving food isn't just a way to stock up for the winter months, but a way to connect with nature and nourish the body and soul.

And so, we present to you our labor of love: an Amish canning and preserving cookbook filled with recipes and wisdom passed down through generations. In this cookbook, you will find not just recipes for delicious jams, jellies, pickles, and more, but also stories and insights from John and me about our respective worlds. Eli will share with you his family's techniques for preserving food, as well as his deep knowledge of farming and the land. I will bring my experience as a physician and healer to bear, with tips and tricks for using food to promote health and well-being.

We hope that this cookbook will inspire you to not just make delicious food, but also to connect with the land, the community, and the traditions around you. We hope that it will help you see the deep connections between food, health, and healing, and that it will encourage you to embrace the simple pleasures of preserving the bounty of the earth. Welcome to our journey of healing through canning and preserving.

Welcome to Amish Canning and Preserving Cookbook

Welcome to Amish Canning and Preserving Cookbook, where the art of preserving food is not just a tradition, but a way of life. Here, you will discover the secrets of the Amish community, passed down from generation to generation, on how to transform fresh, wholesome ingredients into jars of deliciousness that will last you through the seasons.

As you flip through the pages of this cookbook, you will be transported to a world of simplicity, where life moves at a slower pace, and food is prepared with love and care. The Amish take great pride in their gardens, and the fruits and vegetables that they grow are not just sustenance, but a source of joy and pride. It is this same passion that drives them to preserve their bounty, so that they can enjoy the flavors of summer, even in the depths of winter.

But the Amish way of preserving food is not just about practicality. It is also about creating a sense of community and connection. When families come together to can and preserve, it is a time for bonding and sharing stories, passing on knowledge and wisdom from one generation to the next. This cookbook is not just a collection of recipes, but a window into a way of life that values tradition, family, and the simple pleasures of life.

In these pages, you will find recipes for everything from classic jams and jellies to pickles, relishes, and chutneys. You will learn how to can fruits and vegetables, and how to make your own sauces, marinades, and spreads. You will also discover the joy of fermenting, a technique that the Amish have mastered to create tangy, flavorful foods that are good for your gut and your soul.

So, welcome to Amish Canning and Preserving Cookbook. May these recipes bring you as much joy and nourishment as they have brought to generations of Amish families before you. As you create your own jars of goodness, may you feel a sense of connection to the land, to your family, and to the community of canners and preservers who have come before you.

The Importance of Canning and Preserving

Canning and preserving are not just methods of food preservation for the Amish community, they are an art form passed down through generations, a legacy of love and dedication to sustenance and self-sufficiency. The importance of canning and preserving cannot be overstated, for it is the foundation upon which our entire way of life rests.

Every jar of canned tomatoes, every pickled cucumber, every jar of strawberry jam represents not only the bounty of our land but also the hard work and dedication of our community. We take great pride in the process of preserving, from the careful selection of the freshest produce to the meticulous attention to detail during the canning process.

But the importance of canning and preserving goes beyond mere sustenance. It is a way of connecting with our past, of honoring the traditions of our ancestors, and of passing down these skills to future generations. The act of preserving food is an act of love, a way of caring for our families and neighbors, and of ensuring that we have enough to sustain us through the lean times.

Canning and preserving also allow us to enjoy the fruits of our labor long after the harvest season has ended. In the dead of winter, when the fields are barren and the wind howls through the valley, we can still savor the taste of summer in a jar of homemade pickles or a spoonful of homemade jam. It is a reminder that no matter how harsh the winter may be, there is always hope for a bountiful harvest in the coming year.

In a world where processed and packaged food is the norm, the importance of canning and preserving cannot be overstated. It is a way of reclaiming our connection to the land, of preserving the flavors and nutrients of fresh produce, and of preserving the art of cooking from scratch. It is a way of nourishing not only our bodies but also our souls, of connecting with our past and our future, and of celebrating the beauty and bounty of God's creation.

The Amish Philosophy of Food Preservation

In the heart of Amish country, the art of food preservation is an honored tradition that has been passed down through generations. It is more than just a method of keeping food fresh for longer; it is a way of life that reflects the Amish philosophy of simplicity, self-sufficiency, and respect for the earth.

At its core, Amish food preservation is about honoring the abundance of nature and using it to sustain oneself throughout the year. This means taking the time to carefully cultivate and harvest crops, to preserve them in a way that retains their flavor and nutrients, and to share the bounty with one's community. For the Amish, preserving food is not just a necessity, but a joyous celebration of life.

One of the most popular methods of food preservation in the Amish community is canning. Whether it's fruits, vegetables, or meats, the process of canning involves carefully preparing and packing the food in jars, then processing them in a hot water bath to kill any bacteria that might cause spoilage. This method of preserving food allows the Amish to enjoy the fruits of their labor throughout the year, even during the harsh winter months when fresh produce is scarce.

But canning is more than just a practical way to preserve food; it is a reflection of the Amish philosophy of living in harmony with nature. The Amish believe that by preserving food in a way that doesn't require refrigeration or other modern conveniences, they are honoring the natural cycles of life and death that govern the earth. They see themselves as stewards of the land, entrusted with the responsibility of caring for it and using its resources wisely.

This philosophy of food preservation is reflected in every aspect of the Amish way of life. From the way they plant and harvest crops, to the way they prepare and preserve food, the Amish are guided by a deep respect for the earth and a commitment to living in harmony with nature. For them, food preservation is not just a practical necessity, but a sacred act that reflects their most deeply held values.

So whether you're new to the world of canning and preserving or you're an experienced hand, there's much to be learned from the Amish philosophy of food preservation. By taking the time to honor the earth, to savor the flavors of each season, and to share the bounty with those around us, we can all experience the joy and richness of a life lived in harmony with nature.

Canning Safety Guidelines

Canning and preserving is a time-honored tradition that has been passed down through generations in Amish communities. It is a way to savor the fruits of the harvest and the flavors of the season long after they have passed. But with this tradition comes great responsibility, for the safety of those who consume the preserved goods is of utmost importance. Therefore, it is crucial to follow proper canning safety guidelines to ensure that your preserves are not only delicious, but also safe to eat.

First and foremost, always begin with fresh, high-quality ingredients. Whether it be plump tomatoes, crisp cucumbers, or juicy peaches, make sure that they are at the peak of ripeness and free from any signs of decay or spoilage. In addition, it is important to use the correct type of jar for the specific food being canned. A jar with a straight shoulder is best for foods that are liquid or semi-liquid, while a jar with a curved shoulder is better suited for foods that are more solid.

When preparing the jars, be sure to thoroughly wash them in hot, soapy water and inspect them for any cracks or chips. Any jars with defects should not be used, as they can compromise the safety of the preserves. Additionally, it is crucial to properly sterilize the jars and lids before use. This can be done by boiling the jars and lids in a large pot of water for at least 10 minutes.

When filling the jars with the prepared food, it is important to leave the appropriate amount of headspace, as recommended by the recipe. This space allows for proper air circulation, which is necessary for safe canning. It is also important to remove any air bubbles by running a knife or spatula around the inside of the jar before placing the lid on.

Once the jars are filled and the lids are tightly secured, they can be processed in a water bath or pressure canner, depending on the recipe. During processing, it is important to follow the recommended processing time and temperature, as well as the recommended pressure for the specific altitude in which you are canning.

After processing, it is important to allow the jars to cool at room temperature for at least 12 hours before checking the seals. Any jars with unsealed lids should not be consumed, as they may be contaminated and unsafe to eat.

CHAPTER 1: EQUIPMENT AND SUPPLIES

Basic Equipment and Supplies for Canning and Preserving

When it comes to canning and preserving, having the right equipment and supplies is essential to ensuring the success and safety of your preserved foods. As an Amish cook, I know firsthand the importance of proper equipment and supplies, and I want to share my knowledge with you.

One of the most essential pieces of equipment for canning and preserving is a large, heavy-duty stockpot. This pot should be made of high-quality stainless steel or enamel, and should be large enough to hold your canning jars with a few inches of water to cover them. A stockpot with a built-in rack for holding jars is ideal, but if you don't have one, you can purchase a separate canning rack to fit in your pot.

In addition to a stockpot, you'll also need a set of canning jars and lids. Jars come in a variety of sizes, from half-pint to quart, and are typically made of glass. Lids should be new and unused, as reused lids may not seal properly and can cause food spoilage. It's also important to note that jars and lids should be washed in hot, soapy water and sterilized before use.

Another essential piece of equipment for canning and preserving is a set of canning tools. This includes a jar lifter for safely removing jars from hot water, a wide-mouth funnel for filling jars, and a bubble remover for releasing any air bubbles trapped in the jars. You may also find it helpful to have a magnetic lid lifter for removing lids from hot water, and a set of kitchen tongs for handling hot jars.

Finally, don't forget about labels and markers for labeling your preserved foods. It's important to label your jars with the date and contents, so you can keep track of what you've preserved and when it was canned.

When it comes to supplies, you'll need a few basic ingredients for most canning and preserving recipes. These include vinegar, sugar, salt, and pectin. You may also need additional ingredients such as spices, fruits, and vegetables, depending on the recipe you're using.

Types of Canning Jars and Lids

Canning is a traditional preservation method that has been practiced by the Amish community for generations. It involves sealing food in a jar or can and then subjecting it to high heat to kill any bacteria that may cause spoilage. The success of the canning process is highly dependent on the type of canning jars and lids used. In this sub-chapter, we will explore the different types of canning jars and lids commonly used in Amish canning and preserving.

Mason Jars

Mason jars are the most common type of canning jars used in Amish canning and preserving. These jars were originally invented by John L. Mason in 1858, and they have since become a staple in the canning industry. Mason jars come in a variety of sizes, ranging from half-pint to half-gallon, and are made from tempered glass, which can withstand high temperatures without cracking. Mason jars are also equipped with screw-on lids that have a rubber gasket to create a seal. The lids are two-piece, consisting of a flat metal disc and a metal ring that screws onto the jar.

Ball Jars

Ball jars are similar to Mason jars and are also commonly used in Amish canning and preserving. These jars were introduced in 1884 by the Ball Corporation and come in a variety of sizes and shapes. Ball jars are made from high-quality tempered glass, which makes them resistant to heat and breakage. They also come equipped with two-piece lids, consisting of a flat metal disc and a metal ring that screws onto the jar.

Kerr Jars

Kerr jars are another popular type of canning jars used in Amish canning and preserving. These jars were introduced in 1903 by the Kerr Glass Manufacturing Corporation and come in a variety of sizes and shapes. Kerr jars are made from high-quality tempered glass and are designed to withstand high temperatures without cracking. They also come equipped with two-piece lids, consisting of a flat metal disc and a metal ring that screws onto the jar.

Weck Jars

Weck jars are a unique type of canning jar that originated in Germany. These jars are made from thick, tempered glass and feature a glass lid and rubber gasket system that creates an airtight seal. Weck jars are available in a variety of sizes and shapes and are commonly used in Amish canning and preserving for pickling and preserving fruits and vegetables.

Tattler Reusable Canning Lids

Tattler reusable canning lids are a newer type of canning lid that has gained popularity in recent years. These lids are made from BPA-free plastic and feature a rubber gasket that creates an airtight seal. Tattler lids are unique because they are reusable, which makes them a more sustainable option for canning and preserving. They are also dishwasher safe and can be used with any standard Mason jar.

Canning Tools and Accessories

Canning and preserving food is an essential practice in the Amish community. They take pride in the quality and longevity of their canned goods. Canning requires the right tools and accessories to ensure that the food is properly preserved and sealed. In this sub-chapter, we will discuss the various canning tools and accessories that are commonly used in the Amish community.

Canning Jars: Glass canning jars are the preferred choice for canning in the Amish community. They are available in different sizes, including pint, quart, and half-gallon sizes. The jars are designed to withstand high temperatures during the canning process, and they are also durable and long-lasting.

Canning Lids: Canning lids are essential for sealing the jars after the canning process. The Amish community uses two types of canning lids – metal and reusable plastic lids. Metal lids are the most common and are available in regular and wide-mouth sizes. Reusable plastic lids are relatively new in the Amish community, but they are becoming more popular because they are eco-friendly and can be reused for several years.

Canning Bands: Canning bands are used to hold the canning lids in place during the canning process. They are made of metal and are available in regular and wide-mouth sizes.

Canning Tongs: Canning tongs are used to remove the hot jars from the canner. They have a long handle and a gripping mechanism that securely holds the jars without damaging them.

Canning Funnel: A canning funnel is used to fill the jars with food without spilling. The Amish community uses stainless steel or plastic funnels that fit the mouth of the canning jars.

Canning Jar Lifter: A canning jar lifter is a tool that is used to lift the jars in and out of the canner. It has a gripping mechanism that securely holds the jars without causing damage.

Canning Rack: A canning rack is a metal or plastic rack that is used to hold the jars in place during the canning process. It is placed at the bottom of the canner to prevent the jars from touching the bottom of the canner and potentially breaking.

Water Bath Canner: A water bath canner is a large pot that is used to immerse the jars in boiling water during the canning process. The Amish community uses stainless steel or enamel-coated canners that are durable and easy to clean.

Pressure Canner: A pressure canner is used for canning low-acid foods such as vegetables and meats. It uses steam pressure to achieve high temperatures that are necessary for preserving these types of foods. The Amish community uses stainless steel pressure canners that are built to last.

Canning Salt: Canning salt is used to preserve pickles, sauerkraut, and other pickled vegetables. The Amish community uses non-iodized salt because iodized salt can cause discoloration and off-flavors in the preserved foods.

Sources for Canning Supplies

When it comes to canning and preserving, having the right supplies is essential. Whether you're a seasoned canner or just starting out, it's important to know where to find the tools you need to make your preserves successful. In this sub-chapter, we'll explore some of the best sources for canning supplies in an Amish community.

Local Amish Markets

One of the best sources for canning supplies in an Amish community is the local Amish market. These markets often have a wide variety of supplies, including jars, lids, rings, canners, and tools. The advantage of shopping at these markets is that you can often find unique and hard-to-find items that are not available at your typical grocery or hardware store. Additionally, the vendors at these markets are often knowledgeable about canning and preserving and can provide helpful tips and advice.

Online Retailers

In recent years, online retailers have become a popular source for canning supplies. These retailers offer a wide variety of supplies, often at competitive prices. Additionally, shopping online allows you to easily compare prices and product reviews from different sellers, making it easier to find the best deal. Some popular online retailers for canning supplies include Amazon, Walmart, and Lehman's.

Hardware Stores

Hardware stores are another good source for canning supplies. Many of these stores carry a variety of jars, lids, and canning equipment, as well as other supplies like funnels, tongs, and ladles. Some hardware stores even offer classes on canning and preserving, which can be a great way to learn more about the process and meet other canning enthusiasts in your community.

Thrift Stores and Yard Sales

If you're looking for affordable canning supplies, thrift stores and yard sales can be a great option. While the selection may be more limited, you can often find jars, canners, and other tools for a fraction of the cost of buying new. Just be sure to inspect the items carefully before purchasing to ensure they are in good condition and will work properly.

Farm Supply Stores

Farm supply stores are another good source for canning supplies. These stores often carry a variety of jars, lids, and canning equipment, as well as other supplies like pectin, vinegar, and spices. Additionally, many of these stores are located in rural areas where canning and preserving is still a popular practice, so you may be able to find supplies that are specific to your region or community.

Co-ops and Specialty Stores

Co-ops and specialty stores that focus on natural foods and products may also carry canning supplies. These stores often offer a wide selection of jars, lids, and canning equipment, as well as other supplies like organic spices, vinegars, and sweeteners. Additionally, many of these stores may have staff members who are knowledgeable about canning and preserving and can provide advice and support.

There are many sources for canning supplies in an Amish community, including local markets, online retailers, hardware stores, thrift stores and yard sales, farm supply stores, and co-ops and specialty stores.

The key is to shop around and find the best deals and quality products that will help you achieve your canning and preserving goals. With the right supplies and a little bit of knowledge and practice, you can enjoy delicious homemade preserves all year round.

CHAPTER 2: CANNING BASICS

Understanding the Canning Process

The canning process involves placing food in jars, sealing them tightly, and then heating them to a high temperature in order to kill bacteria and other microorganisms that can spoil the food. In this sub-chapter, we will explore the canning process in detail and discuss the various steps involved in preserving food.

Preparation

The first step in canning is to gather all the necessary equipment and ingredients. This includes jars, lids, a canning pot, tongs, a funnel, a ladle, and the food that you wish to can. It is important to select jars and lids that are specifically designed for canning, as other types of jars may not be able to withstand the high temperatures required for the process. Before you begin, make sure that all equipment and jars are thoroughly cleaned and sterilized.

Filling the Jars

Once the equipment is prepared, you can start filling the jars with the food that you wish to preserve. This may include fruits, vegetables, meats, or other types of food. It is important to leave some headspace at the top of the jar to allow for expansion during the canning process. The amount of headspace required will vary depending on the type of food being canned.

Sealing the Jars

After the jars are filled, the next step is to seal them tightly with the lids. This can be done using a canning funnel and a ladle to pour the food into the jars, and then placing the lids on top. The lids should be screwed on firmly but not too tightly, as this can cause the jars to break during the canning process.

Processing the Jars

Once the jars are filled and sealed, they are ready to be processed. This involves placing the jars into a canning pot filled with boiling water, and then boiling them for a set amount of time. The length of time required for processing will depend on the type of food being canned and the altitude at which you are canning. It is important to follow the recipe closely and to use a reliable source of processing times.

Cooling and Storage

After the jars have been processed, they should be removed from the canning pot and allowed to cool at room temperature for 24 hours. During this time, the lids should seal tightly, indicating that the canning process was successful. Once the jars are cool, they can be stored in a cool, dry place for up to a year or more, depending on the type of food being canned.

Overall, the canning process is a time-honored tradition that has been used by the Amish and other communities for centuries to preserve food for long-term storage. By following the steps outlined above and using reliable recipes and processing times, you can ensure that your canned food is safe and delicious for many months to come.

Water Bath Canning vs. Pressure Canning

When it comes to preserving food at home, there are two popular methods that have been used for generations: water bath canning and pressure canning. Both methods have their unique advantages and disadvantages, and the choice of which method to use largely depends on the type of food being preserved.

Water Bath Canning

Water bath canning is a popular method of preserving high-acid foods such as fruits, tomatoes, and pickles. The process involves placing jars of food in a large pot of boiling water for a specified amount of time.

The heat from the boiling water creates a vacuum seal on the jar, preventing air and bacteria from entering and spoiling the food.

One advantage of water bath canning is that it requires minimal equipment and is relatively simple to do. All you need is a large pot, a rack to hold the jars, and a set of canning jars with lids and bands. This makes it an ideal method for beginners who are just starting out with home food preservation.

Another advantage of water bath canning is that it can be done on a stove top, making it accessible to those who do not have access to specialized equipment. Additionally, the process of water bath canning helps to retain the natural color, flavor, and texture of the food being preserved.

However, it is important to note that water bath canning is only suitable for preserving high-acid foods. Low-acid foods such as vegetables, meats, and fish must be preserved using the pressure canning method. This is because the high heat and pressure of pressure canning is necessary to destroy any harmful bacteria that may be present in low-acid foods.

Pressure Canning

Pressure canning is a method of preserving low-acid foods using high heat and pressure. The process involves placing jars of food in a specialized pressure canner and subjecting them to high heat and pressure for a specified amount of time. The high heat and pressure destroy any harmful bacteria present in the food, making it safe for long-term storage.

One advantage of pressure canning is that it can be used to preserve a wide variety of foods, including vegetables, meats, fish, and soups. This makes it a more versatile method of food preservation than water bath canning.

Additionally, pressure canning is the only safe method of preserving low-acid foods. This is because the high heat and pressure of pressure canning is necessary to destroy any harmful bacteria that may be present in low-acid foods. Using water bath canning to preserve low-acid foods can be dangerous and increase the risk of foodborne illness.

However, pressure canning requires specialized equipment, including a pressure canner and a set of canning jars with lids and bands. This can make it a more expensive method of food preservation than water bath canning.

Both water bath canning and pressure canning are effective methods of home food preservation. The choice of which method to use largely depends on the type of food being preserved. Water bath canning is suitable for high-acid foods such as fruits, tomatoes, and pickles, while pressure canning is necessary for low-acid foods such as vegetables, meats, and fish.

Preparing and Packing Jars

Preparing and packing jars correctly is crucial to the success of the canning process. In this sub-chapter, we will cover the steps involved in preparing and packing jars for canning.

Step 1: Selecting Jars

Selecting the right jars for canning is essential. The jars you choose must be specifically designed for canning and preserving. Mason jars are the most popular type of jars used for canning in Amish communities. They come in various sizes, including pint, quart, and half-gallon sizes. Mason jars are made of glass and come with a two-part lid system consisting of a flat metal lid and a screw-on ring.

Before using your jars, ensure that they are free of cracks, chips, and other defects. You should also inspect the lids to ensure that they are not rusted or dented. Any damaged jars or lids should be discarded and replaced with new ones.

Step 2: Cleaning and Sterilizing Jars

Cleaning and sterilizing jars are essential to ensure that the canned food remains safe for consumption. To clean the jars, wash them in hot, soapy water and rinse them thoroughly. You can also run them through a dishwasher on the hottest setting. After washing, sterilize the jars by boiling them in a large pot of water for at least ten minutes. This process kills any bacteria or microorganisms that may be present in the jars.

Step 3: Filling the Jars

Before filling the jars, ensure that the food you are canning is fresh and of high quality. Fill the jars with the food, leaving a half-inch of headspace at the top. Headspace is the distance between the food and the top of the jar. This space is needed to allow for the expansion of the food during the canning process.

Use a funnel to fill the jars, as this makes the process much easier and reduces the risk of spillage. Wipe the rims of the jars with a clean, damp cloth to remove any food residue or spills.

Step 4: Sealing the Jars

Sealing the jars is an essential step in the canning process. To seal the jars, place a flat metal lid on the top of the jar and secure it with a screw-on ring. Tighten the ring just enough to hold the lid in place. Do not over-tighten the ring, as this can prevent air from escaping during the canning process, leading to seal failure.

Step 5: Processing the Jars

After sealing the jars, place them in a large pot of boiling water called a canner. The water level should be at least two inches above the tops of the jars. Boil the jars for the amount of time specified in your recipe. The processing time depends on the type of food being canned and the size of the jars.

Step 6: Cooling and Storing the Jars

After processing, remove the jars from the canner and allow them to cool at room temperature for 24 hours. During this time, you will hear a popping sound as the lids seal. This sound indicates that the jars have been successfully sealed.

After the jars have cooled, remove the screw-on rings and test the seals by pressing down on the center of the lids. If the lids do not move or make a popping sound, the jars are sealed correctly. If any jars are not sealed correctly, refrigerate and consume the food within a few days.

Label the sealed jars with the date and contents and store them in a cool, dry place. Canned food can be stored for up to one year, but it is best to consume it within six months for optimal freshness and flavor.

It is essential to check the jars regularly for signs of spoilage, such as bulging lids, leaking jars, or an off smell. If any of these signs are present, discard the contents of the jar and do not consume it.

CHAPTER 3: AMISH CANNING RECIPES

Introduction to Amish Canning Recipes

Amish canning recipes are typically passed down from generation to generation and are characterized by their simplicity, practicality, and reliance on natural ingredients. These recipes often involve using traditional techniques, such as water bath canning or pressure canning, to ensure that the food is safely preserved for long periods.

One of the most popular Amish canning recipes is for dill pickles, which are made with cucumbers, fresh dill, garlic, and pickling spices. The pickles are first washed and trimmed before being packed tightly into jars with the other ingredients. The jars are then filled with a brine made from vinegar, water, and salt before being processed in a water bath canner for several minutes. The result is a crunchy, tangy pickle that can be enjoyed throughout the year.

Another beloved Amish canning recipe is for apple butter, a smooth and creamy spread made from cooked and pureed apples, sugar, and spices such as cinnamon and nutmeg. The apples are first peeled, cored, and chopped before being cooked down with the other ingredients until they reach a thick, spreadable consistency. The apple butter is then packed into jars and processed in a water bath canner for 10-15 minutes to ensure that it is safely preserved.

Amish canning recipes are not limited to pickles and apple butter, however. Other popular recipes include canned tomatoes, green beans, peaches, and a variety of jams and jellies made from fresh berries and fruits. These recipes are often simple and rely on the natural sweetness and flavor of the ingredients.

It is worth noting that while Amish canning recipes have been used for generations, it is important to follow modern canning guidelines to ensure that the food is safely preserved. This includes using properly sterilized jars and lids, following recommended processing times and temperatures, and avoiding outdated canning techniques that may be unsafe.

Canned Fruits Recipes:

CANNED PEACHES:

Ingredients:

- 8 lbs of peaches
- 4 cups of granulated sugar
- 8 cups of water

Instructions:

- Peel and slice peaches. Remove pits.
- Combine sugar and water in a large pot and bring to a boil.
- Add peaches to the boiling syrup and cook for 5 minutes.
- Pack peaches into hot jars, leaving 1/2 inch headspace.
- Pour hot syrup over peaches, leaving 1/2 inch headspace.
- Remove air bubbles, wipe jar rims, and seal jars.
- Process jars in a boiling water canner for 25 minutes.

CANNED PEARS:

Ingredients:

- 8 lbs of pears
- 4 cups of granulated sugar
- 8 cups of water
- 2 cinnamon sticks

Instructions:

- Peel and slice pears. Remove cores.
- Combine sugar, water, and cinnamon sticks in a large pot and bring to a boil.
- Add pears to the boiling syrup and cook for 5 minutes.

- Pack pears into hot jars, leaving 1/2 inch headspace.
- Pour hot syrup over pears, leaving 1/2 inch headspace.
- Remove air bubbles, wipe jar rims, and seal jars.
- Process jars in a boiling water canner for 20 minutes.

CANNED APPLESAUCE:

Ingredients:

- 8 lbs of apples
- 4 cups of water
- 1 cup of granulated sugar
- 1 tablespoon of lemon juice
- 2 cinnamon sticks

Instructions:

- Peel, core, and slice apples.
- Combine apples, water, sugar, lemon juice, and cinnamon sticks in a large pot and bring to a boil.
- Reduce heat and simmer for 30 minutes or until apples are soft.
- Remove cinnamon sticks and blend apples until smooth.
- Pack applesauce into hot jars, leaving 1/2 inch headspace.
- Remove air bubbles, wipe jar rims, and seal jars.
- Process jars in a boiling water canner for 20 minutes.

CANNED CHERRIES:

Ingredients:

- 8 lbs of cherries
- 4 cups of granulated sugar
- 4 cups of water

- 1 tablespoon of lemon juice

Instructions:

- Remove pits from cherries.
- Combine sugar, water, and lemon juice in a large pot and bring to a boil.
- Add cherries to the boiling syrup and cook for 5 minutes.
- Pack cherries into hot jars, leaving 1/2 inch headspace.
- Pour hot syrup over cherries, leaving 1/2 inch headspace.
- Remove air bubbles, wipe jar rims, and seal jars.
- Process jars in a boiling water canner for 15 minutes.

CANNED PINEAPPLE:

Ingredients:

- 8 lbs of pineapple
- 4 cups of granulated sugar
- 8 cups of water

Instructions:

- Peel and slice pineapple. Remove core.
- Combine sugar and water in a large pot and bring to a boil.
- Add pineapple to the boiling syrup and cook for 10 minutes.
- Pack pineapple into hot jars, leaving 1/2 inch headspace.
- Pour hot syrup over pineapple, leaving 1/2 inch headspace.
- Remove air bubbles, wipe jar rims, and seal jars.
- Process jars in a boiling water canner for 20 minutes.

CANNED APRICOTS:

Ingredients:

- 8 lbs of apricots
- 4 cups of granulated sugar
- 4 cups of water

Instructions:

- Peel and slice apricots. Remove pits.
- Combine sugar and water in a large pot and bring to a boil.
- Add apricots to the boiling syrup and cook for 5 minutes.
- Pack apricots into hot jars, leaving 1/2 inch headspace.
- Pour hot syrup over apricots, leaving 1/2 inch headspace.
- Remove air bubbles, wipe jar rims, and seal jars.
- Process jars in a boiling water canner for 20 minutes.

CANNED PLUMS:

Ingredients:

- 8 lbs of plums
- 4 cups of granulated sugar
- 4 cups of water
- 1 tablespoon of lemon juice

Instructions:

- Peel and slice plums. Remove pits.
- Combine sugar, water, and lemon juice in a large pot and bring to a boil.
- Add plums to the boiling syrup and cook for 5 minutes.
- Pack plums into hot jars, leaving 1/2 inch headspace.
- Pour hot syrup over plums, leaving 1/2 inch headspace.
- Remove air bubbles, wipe jar rims, and seal jars.
- Process jars in a boiling water canner for 20 minutes.

CANNED NECTARINES:

Ingredients:

- 8 lbs of nectarines
- 4 cups of granulated sugar
- 4 cups of water

Instructions:

- Peel and slice nectarines. Remove pits.
- Combine sugar and water in a large pot and bring to a boil.
- Add nectarines to the boiling syrup and cook for 5 minutes.
- Pack nectarines into hot jars, leaving 1/2 inch headspace.
- Pour hot syrup over nectarines, leaving 1/2 inch headspace.
- Remove air bubbles, wipe jar rims, and seal jars.
- Process jars in a boiling water canner for 20 minutes.

CANNED STRAWBERRIES:

Ingredients:

- 8 lbs of strawberries
- 4 cups of granulated sugar
- 4 cups of water
- 1 tablespoon of lemon juice

Instructions:

- Hull strawberries and cut into halves or quarters.
- Combine sugar, water, and lemon juice in a large pot and bring to a boil.
- Add strawberries to the boiling syrup and cook for 5 minutes.
- Pack strawberries into hot jars, leaving 1/2 inch headspace.
- Pour hot syrup over strawberries, leaving 1/2 inch headspace.

- Remove air bubbles, wipe jar rims, and seal jars.
- Process jars in a boiling water canner for 15 minutes.

CANNED BLUEBERRIES:

Ingredients:

- 8 lbs of blueberries
- 4 cups of granulated sugar
- 4 cups of water
- 1 tablespoon of lemon juice

Instructions:

- Rinse blueberries and remove stems.
- Combine sugar, water, and lemon juice in a large pot and bring to a boil.
- Add blueberries to the boiling syrup and cook for 5 minutes.
- Pack blueberries into hot jars, leaving 1/2 inch headspace.
- Pour hot syrup over blueberries, leaving 1/2 inch headspace.
- Remove air bubbles, wipe jar rims, and seal jars.
- Process jars in a boiling water canner for 15 minutes.

CANNED RASPBERRIES:

Ingredients:

- 8 lbs of raspberries
- 4 cups of granulated sugar
- 4 cups of water
- 1 tablespoon of lemon juice

Instructions:

- Rinse raspberries and remove any stems or leaves.

- Combine sugar, water, and lemon juice in a large pot and bring to a boil.

- Add raspberries to the boiling syrup and cook for 5 minutes.

- Pack raspberries into hot jars, leaving 1/2 inch headspace.

- Pour hot syrup over raspberries, leaving 1/2 inch headspace.

- Remove air bubbles, wipe jar rims, and seal jars.

- Process jars in a boiling water canner for 15 minutes.

CANNED BLACKBERRIES:

Ingredients:

- 8 lbs of blackberries

- 4 cups of granulated sugar

- 4 cups of water

- 1 tablespoon of lemon juice

Instructions:

- Rinse blackberries and remove any stems or leaves.

- Combine sugar, water, and lemon juice in a large pot and bring to a boil.

- Add blackberries to the boiling syrup and cook for 5 minutes.

- Pack blackberries into hot jars, leaving 1/2 inch headspace.

- Pour hot syrup over blackberries, leaving 1/2 inch headspace.

- Remove air bubbles, wipe jar rims, and seal jars.

- Process jars in a boiling water canner for 15 minutes.

CANNED MANGOES:

Ingredients:

- 8 lbs of mangoes

- 4 cups of granulated sugar

- 4 cups of water
- 1 tablespoon of lemon juice

Instructions:

- Peel and dice mangoes.
- Combine sugar, water, and lemon juice in a large pot and bring to a boil.
- Add mangoes to the boiling syrup and cook for 5 minutes.
- Pack mangoes into hot jars, leaving 1/2 inch headspace.
- Pour hot syrup over mangoes, leaving 1/2 inch headspace.
- Remove air bubbles, wipe jar rims, and seal jars.
- Process jars in a boiling water canner for 20 minutes.

CANNED KIWIS:

Ingredients:

- 8 lbs of kiwis
- 4 cups of granulated sugar
- 4 cups of water
- 1 tablespoon of lemon juice

Instructions:

- Peel and slice kiwis.
- Combine sugar, water, and lemon juice in a large pot and bring to a boil.
- Add kiwis to the boiling syrup and cook for 5 minutes.
- Pack kiwis into hot jars, leaving 1/2 inch headspace.
- Pour hot syrup over kiwis, leaving 1/2 inch headspace.
- Remove air bubbles, wipe jar rims, and seal jars.
- Process jars in a boiling water canner for 20 minutes.

CANNED GRAPEFRUIT:

Ingredients:

- 8 lbs of grapefruit
- 4 cups of granulated sugar
- 4 cups of water

Instructions:

- Peel grapefruit and remove membranes. Cut into sections.
- Combine sugar and water in a large pot and bring to a boil.
- Add grapefruit sections to the boiling syrup and cook for 5 minutes.
- Pack grapefruit sections into hot jars, leaving 1/2 inch headspace.
- Pour hot syrup over grapefruit sections, leaving 1/2 inch headspace.
- Remove air bubbles, wipe jar rims, and seal jars.
- Process jars in a boiling water canner for 15 minutes.

CANNED ORANGES:

Ingredients:

- 8 lbs of oranges
- 4 cups of granulated sugar
- 4 cups of water

Instructions:

- Peel oranges and remove membranes. Cut into sections.
- Combine sugar and water in a large pot and bring to a boil.
- Add orange sections to the boiling syrup and cook for 5 minutes.
- Pack orange sections into hot jars, leaving 1/2 inch headspace.
- Pour hot syrup over orange sections, leaving 1/2 inch headspace.
- Remove air bubbles, wipe jar rims, and seal jars.

- Process jars in a boiling water canner for 15 minutes.

CANNED MANDARIN ORANGES:

Ingredients:

- 8 lbs of mandarin oranges
- 4 cups of granulated sugar
- 4 cups of water

Instructions:

- Peel mandarin oranges and remove membranes. Cut into sections.
- Combine sugar and water in a large pot and bring to a boil.
- Add mandarin orange sections to the boiling syrup and cook for 5 minutes.
- Pack mandarin orange sections into hot jars, leaving 1/2 inch headspace.
- Pour hot syrup over mandarin orange sections, leaving 1/2 inch headspace.
- Remove air bubbles, wipe jar rims, and seal jars.
- Process jars in a boiling water canner for 15 minutes.

CANNED FIGS:

Ingredients:

- 8 lbs of figs
- 4 cups of granulated sugar
- 4 cups of water
- 1 tablespoon of lemon juice

Instructions:

- Rinse figs and remove stems. Cut into quarters.
- Combine sugar, water, and lemon juice in a large pot and bring to a boil.
- Add figs to the boiling syrup and cook for 5 minutes.

- Pack figs into hot jars, leaving 1/2 inch headspace.

- Pour hot syrup over figs, leaving 1/2 inch headspace.

- Remove air bubbles, wipe jar rims, and seal jars.

- Process jars in a boiling water canner for 20 minutes.

CANNED PRUNES:

Ingredients:

- 8 lbs of prunes

- 4 cups of granulated sugar

- 4 cups of water

Instructions:

- Rinse prunes and remove pits. Cut into halves.

- Combine sugar and water in a large pot and bring to a boil.

- Add prunes to the boiling syrup and cook for 5 minutes.

- Pack prunes into hot jars, leaving 1/2 inch headspace.

- Pour hot syrup over prunes, leaving 1/2 inch headspace.

- Remove air bubbles, wipe jar rims, and seal jars.

- Process jars in a boiling water canner for 20 minutes.

CANNED WATERMELON RIND:

Ingredients:

- 8 lbs of watermelon rind

- 4 cups of granulated sugar

- 4 cups of water

- 2 cups of vinegar

- 1 cinnamon stick

- 1 teaspoon of whole cloves
- 1 teaspoon of allspice berries

Instructions:

- Peel green outer layer of watermelon rind and discard. Cut remaining white rind into 1 inch pieces.
- Combine sugar, water, vinegar, cinnamon stick, cloves, and allspice berries in a large pot and bring to a boil.
- Add watermelon rind to the boiling syrup and cook for 30 minutes.
- Pack watermelon rind into hot jars, leaving 1/2 inch headspace.
- Pour hot syrup over watermelon rind, leaving 1/2 inch headspace.
- Remove air bubbles, wipe jar rims, and seal jars.
- Process jars in a boiling water canner for 10 minutes.

Notes: *This canned watermelon rind can be used as a side dish or in recipes that call for pickled watermelon rind. Store in a cool, dry place and use within one year.*

Overall, canning fruits is a great way to preserve them for later use. With these recipes, you can enjoy the flavors of your favorite fruits all year round. Just remember to follow safe canning practices and enjoy the fruits of your labor!

Canned Vegetables Recipes:

CANNED TOMATOES

Ingredients:

- Fresh, ripe tomatoes
- Water
- Lemon juice (optional)

Instructions:

- Start by washing the tomatoes in cold water and removing the stem.
- Blanch the tomatoes by boiling them in a pot of water for 30-60 seconds, then immediately transfer them to a bowl of ice water.
- Once cooled, peel the skins off the tomatoes and cut them into halves or quarters.
- Place the tomatoes into sterilized canning jars, leaving about 1 inch of headspace.
- Pour boiling water over the tomatoes, ensuring they are fully covered, and add 1 tablespoon of lemon juice to each quart jar (if desired).
- Remove any air bubbles and adjust the headspace as needed.
- Place the lids and bands on the jars, and process them in a pressure canner for 85 minutes for pints or 90 minutes for quarts.
- Allow the jars to cool, and then check to ensure they are properly sealed. Store in a cool, dry place.

CANNED GREEN BEANS

Ingredients:

- Fresh green beans
- Water
- Salt

Instructions:

- Wash the green beans in cold water and remove any stems or ends.
- Cut the beans to desired length.
- Place the beans into sterilized canning jars, leaving about 1 inch of headspace.
- Pour boiling water over the beans, ensuring they are fully covered, and add 1/2 teaspoon of salt to each pint jar (or 1 teaspoon per quart).
- Remove any air bubbles and adjust the headspace as needed.
- Place the lids and bands on the jars, and process them in a pressure canner for 20 minutes for pints or 25 minutes for quarts.
- Allow the jars to cool, and then check to ensure they are properly sealed. Store in a cool, dry place.

CANNED CORN

Ingredients:

- Fresh corn
- Water
- Salt

Instructions:

- Husk and clean the corn.
- Cut the kernels off the cob.
- Place the corn into sterilized canning jars, leaving about 1 inch of headspace.
- Pour boiling water over the corn, ensuring they are fully covered, and add 1/2 teaspoon of salt to each pint jar (or 1 teaspoon per quart).
- Remove any air bubbles and adjust the headspace as needed.
- Place the lids and bands on the jars, and process them in a pressure canner for 85 minutes for pints or 90 minutes for quarts.
- Allow the jars to cool, and then check to ensure they are properly sealed. Store in a cool, dry place.

CANNED CARROTS

Ingredients:

- Fresh carrots
- Water

Instructions:

- Peel and wash the carrots.
- Cut them into desired sizes.
- Place the carrots into sterilized canning jars, leaving about 1 inch of headspace.
- Pour boiling water over the carrots, ensuring they are fully covered.

- Remove any air bubbles and adjust the headspace as needed.
- Place the lids and bands on the jars, and process them in a pressure canner for 25 minutes for pints or 30 minutes for quarts.
- Allow the jars to cool, and then check to ensure they are properly sealed. Store in a cool, dry place.

CANNED BEETS

Ingredients:

- Fresh beets
- Water
- Vinegar
- Salt

Instructions:

- Peel and wash the beets.
- Cut them into desired sizes.
- Place the beets into sterilized canning jars, leaving about 1 inch of headspace.
- In a separate pot, mix together 2 cups of water, 1 cup of vinegar, and 1 teaspoon of salt, and bring to a boil.
- Pour the mixture over the beets in the jars, ensuring they are fully covered.
- Remove any air bubbles and adjust the headspace as needed.
- Place the lids and bands on the jars, and process them in a pressure canner for 30 minutes for pints or 35 minutes for quarts.
- Allow the jars to cool, and then check to ensure they are properly sealed. Store in a cool, dry place.

CANNED SQUASH

Ingredients:

- Fresh squash
- Water

- Salt

Instructions:

- Wash the squash and cut it into desired sizes.
- Place the squash into sterilized canning jars, leaving about 1 inch of headspace.
- Pour boiling water over the squash, ensuring they are fully covered, and add 1/2 teaspoon of salt to each pint jar (or 1 teaspoon per quart).
- Remove any air bubbles and adjust the headspace as needed.
- Place the lids and bands on the jars, and process them in a pressure canner for 25 minutes for pints or 30 minutes for quarts.
- Allow the jars to cool, and then check to ensure they are properly sealed. Store in a cool, dry place.

CANNED PEAS

Ingredients:

- Fresh peas
- Water
- Salt
- Instructions:
- Wash the peas in cold water and remove any stems or pods.
- Place the peas into sterilized canning jars, leaving about 1 inch of headspace.
- Pour boiling water over the peas, ensuring they are fully covered, and add 1/2 teaspoon of salt to each pint jar (or 1 teaspoon per quart).
- Remove any air bubbles and adjust the headspace as needed.
- Place the lids and bands on the jars, and process them in a pressure canner for 40 minutes for pints or 45 minutes for quarts.
- Allow the jars to cool, and then check to ensure they are properly sealed. Store in a cool, dry place.

CANNED ASPARAGUS

Ingredients:

- Fresh asparagus
- Water
- Salt

Instructions:

- Wash the asparagus and trim the woody ends.
- Cut the asparagus to fit into sterilized canning jars, leaving about 1 inch of headspace.
- Pour boiling water over the asparagus, ensuring they are fully covered, and add 1/2 teaspoon of salt to each pint jar (or 1 teaspoon per quart).
- Remove any air bubbles and adjust the headspace as needed.
- Place the lids and bands on the jars, and process them in a pressure canner for 30 minutes for pints or 35 minutes for quarts.
- Allow the jars to cool, and then check to ensure they are properly sealed. Store in a cool, dry place.

CANNED OKRA

Ingredients:

- Fresh okra
- Water
- Vinegar
- Salt

Instructions:

- Wash the okra and trim the ends.
- Place the okra into sterilized canning jars, leaving about 1 inch of headspace.
- In a separate pot, mix together 2 cups of water, 1 cup of vinegar, and 1 teaspoon of salt, and bring to a boil.
- Pour the mixture over the okra in the jars, ensuring they are fully covered.
- Remove any air bubbles and adjust the headspace as needed.

- Place the lids and bands on the jars, and process them in a pressure canner for 25 minutes for pints or 30 minutes for quarts.
- Allow the jars to cool, and then check to ensure they are properly sealed. Store in a cool, dry place.

CANNED TURNIPS

Ingredients:

- Fresh turnips
- Water
- Salt

Instructions:

- Wash the turnips and peel them.
- Cut the turnips into desired sizes and place them into sterilized canning jars, leaving about 1 inch of headspace.
- Pour boiling water over the turnips, ensuring they are fully covered, and add 1/2 teaspoon of salt to each pint jar (or 1 teaspoon per quart).
- Remove any air bubbles and adjust the headspace as needed.
- Place the lids and bands on the jars, and process them in a pressure canner for 25 minutes for pints or 30 minutes for quarts.
- Allow the jars to cool, and then check to ensure they are properly sealed. Store in a cool, dry place.

CANNED SWEET POTATOES

Ingredients:

- Fresh sweet potatoes
- Water

Instructions:

- Wash the sweet potatoes and peel them.

- Cut the sweet potatoes into desired sizes and place them into sterilized canning jars, leaving about 1 inch of headspace.
- Pour boiling water over the sweet potatoes, ensuring they are fully covered.
- Remove any air bubbles and adjust the headspace as needed.
- Place the lids and bands on the jars, and process them in a pressure canner for 90 minutes for pints or quarts.
- Allow the jars to cool, and then check to ensure they are properly sealed. Store in a cool, dry place.

CANNED POTATOES

Ingredients:

- Fresh potatoes
- Water
- Salt

Instructions:

- Wash the potatoes and peel them.
- Cut the potatoes into desired sizes and place them into sterilized canning jars, leaving about 1 inch of headspace.
- Pour boiling water over the potatoes, ensuring they are fully covered, and add 1/2 teaspoon of salt to each pint jar (or 1 teaspoon per quart).
- Remove any air bubbles and adjust the headspace as needed.
- Place the lids and bands on the jars, and process them in a pressure canner for 35 minutes for pints or 40 minutes for quarts.
- Allow the jars to cool, and then check to ensure they are properly sealed. Store in a cool, dry place.

CANNED LIMA BEANS

Ingredients:

- Fresh lima beans

- Water
- Salt

Instructions:

- Wash the lima beans in cold water and remove any stems or pods.
- Place the lima beans into sterilized canning jars, leaving about 1 inch of headspace.
- Pour boiling water over the lima beans, ensuring they are fully covered, and add 1/2 teaspoon of salt to each pint jar (or 1 teaspoon per quart).
- Remove any air bubbles and adjust the headspace as needed.
- Place the lids and bands on the jars, and process them in a pressure canner for 40 minutes for pints or 45 minutes for quarts.
- Allow the jars to cool, and then check to ensure they are properly sealed. Store in a cool, dry place.

CANNED CABBAGE

Ingredients:

- Fresh cabbage
- Water
- Salt

Instructions:

- Wash the cabbage and remove the outer leaves.
- Cut the cabbage into desired sizes and place them into sterilized canning jars, leaving about 1 inch of headspace.
- Pour boiling water over the cabbage, ensuring they are fully covered, and add 1/2 teaspoon of salt to each pint jar (or 1 teaspoon per quart).
- Remove any air bubbles and adjust the headspace as needed.
- Place the lids and bands on the jars, and process them in a pressure canner for 90 minutes for pints or quarts.
- Allow the jars to cool, and then check to ensure they are properly sealed. Store in a cool, dry place.

CANNED BRUSSELS SPROUTS

Ingredients:

- Fresh Brussels sprouts
- Water
- Salt

Instructions:

- Wash the Brussels sprouts and remove any loose outer leaves.
- Cut off the ends of the Brussels sprouts and place them into sterilized canning jars, leaving about 1 inch of headspace.
- Pour boiling water over the Brussels sprouts, ensuring they are fully covered, and add 1/2 teaspoon of salt to each pint jar (or 1 teaspoon per quart).
- Remove any air bubbles and adjust the headspace as needed.
- Place the lids and bands on the jars, and process them in a pressure canner for 90 minutes for pints or quarts.
- Allow the jars to cool, and then check to ensure they are properly sealed. Store in a cool, dry place.

CANNED CAULIFLOWER

Ingredients:

- Fresh cauliflower
- Water
- Salt
- Lemon juice (optional)

Instructions:

- Wash the cauliflower and cut it into florets.
- Place the cauliflower florets into sterilized canning jars, leaving about 1 inch of headspace.

- Pour boiling water over the cauliflower, ensuring they are fully covered, and add 1/2 teaspoon of salt to each pint jar (or 1 teaspoon per quart). Optionally, add 1 tablespoon of lemon juice to each jar to help preserve color.
- Remove any air bubbles and adjust the headspace as needed.
- Place the lids and bands on the jars, and process them in a pressure canner for 10 minutes for pints or 15 minutes for quarts.
- Allow the jars to cool, and then check to ensure they are properly sealed. Store in a cool, dry place.

CANNED BROCCOLI

Ingredients:

- Fresh broccoli
- Water
- Salt
- Lemon juice (optional)

Instructions:

- Wash the broccoli and cut it into florets.
- Place the broccoli florets into sterilized canning jars, leaving about 1 inch of headspace.
- Pour boiling water over the broccoli, ensuring they are fully covered, and add 1/2 teaspoon of salt to each pint jar (or 1 teaspoon per quart). Optionally, add 1 tablespoon of lemon juice to each jar to help preserve color.
- Remove any air bubbles and adjust the headspace as needed.
- Place the lids and bands on the jars, and process them in a pressure canner for 10 minutes for pints or 15 minutes for quarts.
- Allow the jars to cool, and then check to ensure they are properly sealed. Store in a cool, dry place.

CANNED PEPPERS

Ingredients:

- Fresh peppers (any variety)
- Water
- Vinegar
- Salt

Instructions:

- Wash the peppers and remove the stems and seeds.
- Cut the peppers into desired sizes and place them into sterilized canning jars, leaving about 1 inch of headspace.
- In a separate pot, bring equal parts water and vinegar to a boil. Add 1/2 teaspoon of salt to each pint jar (or 1 teaspoon per quart) of peppers.
- Pour the hot water and vinegar mixture over the peppers, ensuring they are fully covered.
- Remove any air bubbles and adjust the headspace as needed.
- Place the lids and bands on the jars, and process them in a water bath canner for 15 minutes for pints or 20 minutes for quarts.
- Allow the jars to cool, and then check to ensure they are properly sealed. Store in a cool, dry place.

CANNED EGGPLANT

Ingredients:

- Fresh eggplant
- Water
- Vinegar
- Salt

Instructions:

- Wash the eggplant and slice it into desired sizes.
- Place the eggplant slices into sterilized canning jars, leaving about 1 inch of headspace.
- In a separate pot, bring equal parts water and vinegar to a boil. Add 1/2 teaspoon of salt to each pint jar (or 1 teaspoon per quart) of eggplant.

- Pour the hot water and vinegar mixture over the eggplant, ensuring they are fully covered.

- Remove any air bubbles and adjust the headspace as needed.

- Place the lids and bands on the jars, and process them in a water bath canner for 40 minutes for pints or quarts.

- Allow the jars to cool, and then check to ensure they are properly sealed. Store in a cool, dry place.

CANNED ZUCCHINI

Ingredients:

- Fresh zucchini
- Water
- Salt
- Lemon juice (optional)

Instructions:

- Wash the zucchini and slice it into desired sizes.

- Place the zucchini slices into sterilized canning jars, leaving about 1 inch of headspace.

- Pour boiling water over the zucchini, ensuring they are fully covered, and add 1/2 teaspoon of salt to each pint jar (or 1 teaspoon per quart). Optionally, add 1 tablespoon of lemon juice to each jar to help preserve color.

- Remove any air bubbles and adjust the headspace as needed.

- Place the lids and bands on the jars, and process them in a pressure canner for 30 minutes for pints or 35 minutes for quarts.

- Allow the jars to cool, and then check to ensure they are properly sealed. Store in a cool, dry place.

Jellies and Jams Recipes:

STRAWBERRY JAM

Ingredients:

- 4 cups of fresh strawberries
- 4 cups of granulated sugar
- 1/4 cup of lemon juice
- 1 package of pectin

Directions:

- Wash and hull the strawberries.
- Crush the berries in a large pot using a potato masher.
- Mix the pectin with 1/4 cup of sugar in a separate bowl.
- Add the pectin mixture to the crushed berries and stir well.
- Add the remaining sugar and lemon juice to the pot and bring to a boil over high heat.
- Stir frequently and let the mixture boil for 1 minute.
- Remove from heat and skim any foam from the surface of the jam.
- Ladle the jam into sterilized jars, leaving 1/4 inch of headspace.
- Wipe the rims of the jars clean and seal with lids and bands.
- Process in a boiling water canner for 10 minutes.

BLUEBERRY JAM

Ingredients:

- 5 cups of fresh blueberries
- 4 cups of granulated sugar
- 1/4 cup of lemon juice
- 1 package of pectin

Directions:

- Wash the blueberries and remove any stems.
- Crush the berries in a large pot using a potato masher.
- Mix the pectin with 1/4 cup of sugar in a separate bowl.

- Add the pectin mixture to the crushed blueberries and stir well.

- Add the remaining sugar and lemon juice to the pot and bring to a boil over high heat.

- Stir frequently and let the mixture boil for 1 minute.

- Remove from heat and skim any foam from the surface of the jam.

- Ladle the jam into sterilized jars, leaving 1/4 inch of headspace.

- Wipe the rims of the jars clean and seal with lids and bands.

- Process in a boiling water canner for 10 minutes.

RASPBERRY JAM

Ingredients:

- 4 cups of fresh raspberries

- 4 cups of granulated sugar

- 1/4 cup of lemon juice

- 1 package of pectin

Directions:

- Wash the raspberries and remove any stems.

- Crush the berries in a large pot using a potato masher.

- Mix the pectin with 1/4 cup of sugar in a separate bowl.

- Add the pectin mixture to the crushed raspberries and stir well.

- Add the remaining sugar and lemon juice to the pot and bring to a boil over high heat.

- Stir frequently and let the mixture boil for 1 minute.

- Remove from heat and skim any foam from the surface of the jam.

- Ladle the jam into sterilized jars, leaving 1/4 inch of headspace.

- Wipe the rims of the jars clean and seal with lids and bands.

- Process in a boiling water canner for 10 minutes.

BLACKBERRY JAM

Ingredients:

- 4 cups of fresh blackberries
- 4 cups of granulated sugar
- 1/4 cup of lemon juice
- 1 package of pectin

Directions:

- Wash the blackberries and remove any stems.
- Crush the berries in a large pot using a potato masher.
- Mix the pectin with 1/4 cup of sugar in a separate bowl.
- Add the pectin mixture to the crushed blackberries and stir well.
- Add the remaining sugar and lemon juice to the pot and bring to a boil over high heat.
- Stir frequently and let the mixture boil for 1 minute.
- Remove from heat and skim any foam from the surface of the jam.
- Ladle the jam into sterilized jars, leaving 1/4 inch of headspace.
- Wipe the rims of the jars clean and seal with lids and bands.
- Process in a boiling water canner for 10 minutes.

GRAPE JELLY

Ingredients:

- 5 cups of fresh grapes (concord or muscadine)
- 4 cups of granulated sugar
- 1/4 cup of lemon juice
- 1 package of pectin

Directions:

- Wash the grapes and remove any stems.
- In a large pot, crush the grapes and add enough water to cover them.
- Bring the mixture to a boil over high heat and then reduce to a simmer for 10 minutes.

- Strain the grape juice through a fine-mesh sieve or cheesecloth.

- Measure 4 cups of the grape juice into a pot.

- Mix the pectin with 1/4 cup of sugar in a separate bowl.

- Add the pectin mixture to the grape juice and stir well.

- Add the remaining sugar and lemon juice to the pot and bring to a boil over high heat.

- Stir frequently and let the mixture boil for 1 minute.

- Remove from heat and skim any foam from the surface of the jelly.

- Ladle the jelly into sterilized jars, leaving 1/4 inch of headspace.

- Wipe the rims of the jars clean and seal with lids and bands.

- Process in a boiling water canner for 10 minutes.

PEACH JELLY

Ingredients:

- 5 cups of ripe peaches

- 4 cups of granulated sugar

- 1/4 cup of lemon juice

- 1 package of pectin

Directions:

- Wash, peel, and pit the peaches.

- Chop the peaches into small pieces and place them in a large pot.

- Add enough water to cover the peaches and bring to a boil over high heat.

- Reduce heat and simmer for 10 minutes.

- Strain the peach juice through a fine-mesh sieve or cheesecloth.

- Measure 4 cups of the peach juice into a pot.

- Mix the pectin with 1/4 cup of sugar in a separate bowl.

- Add the pectin mixture to the peach juice and stir well.

- Add the remaining sugar and lemon juice to the pot and bring to a boil over high heat.

- Stir frequently and let the mixture boil for 1 minute.

- Remove from heat and skim any foam from the surface of the jelly.
- Ladle the jelly into sterilized jars, leaving 1/4 inch of headspace.
- Wipe the rims of the jars clean and seal with lids and bands.
- Process in a boiling water canner for 10 minutes.

APPLE JELLY

Ingredients:

- 5 cups of apples, chopped (use tart apples like Granny Smith)
- 4 cups of granulated sugar
- 1/4 cup of lemon juice
- 1 package of pectin

Directions:

- Wash and chop the apples into small pieces, leaving the skin and cores intact.
- Place the apples in a large pot and add enough water to cover them.
- Bring the mixture to a boil over high heat and then reduce to a simmer for 20-25 minutes.
- Strain the apple juice through a fine-mesh sieve or cheesecloth.
- Measure 4 cups of the apple juice into a pot.
- Mix the pectin with 1/4 cup of sugar in a separate bowl.
- Add the pectin mixture to the apple juice and stir well.
- Add the remaining sugar and lemon juice to the pot and bring to a boil over high heat.
- Stir frequently and let the mixture boil for 1 minute.
- Remove from heat and skim any foam from the surface of the jelly.
- Ladle the jelly into sterilized jars, leaving 1/4 inch of headspace.
- Wipe the rims of the jars clean and seal with lids and bands.
- Process in a boiling water canner for 10 minutes.

PLUM JELLY

Ingredients:

- 5 cups of ripe plums, chopped
- 4 cups of granulated sugar
- 1/4 cup of lemon juice
- 1 package of pectin

Directions:

- Wash and chop the plums into small pieces, leaving the skins and pits intact.
- Place the plums in a large pot and add enough water to cover them.
- Bring the mixture to a boil over high heat and then reduce to a simmer for 20-25 minutes.
- Strain the plum juice through a fine-mesh sieve or cheesecloth.
- Measure 4 cups of the plum juice into a pot.
- Mix the pectin with 1/4 cup of sugar in a separate bowl.
- Add the pectin mixture to the plum juice and stir well.
- Add the remaining sugar and lemon juice to the pot and bring to a boil over high heat.
- Stir frequently and let the mixture boil for 1 minute.
- Remove from heat and skim any foam from the surface of the jelly.
- Ladle the jelly into sterilized jars, leaving 1/4 inch of headspace.
- Wipe the rims of the jars clean and seal with lids and bands.
- Process in a boiling water canner for 10 minutes.

QUINCE JELLY

Ingredients:

- 5 cups of quince, chopped
- 4 cups of granulated sugar
- 1/4 cup of lemon juice
- 1 package of pectin

Directions:

- Wash and chop the quince into small pieces, leaving the skin and seeds intact.

- Place the quince in a large pot and add enough water to cover them.

- Bring the mixture to a boil over high heat and then reduce to a simmer for 20-25 minutes.

- Strain the quince juice through a fine-mesh sieve or cheesecloth.

- Measure 4 cups of the quince juice into a pot.

- Mix the pectin with 1/4 cup of sugar in a separate bowl.

- Add the pectin mixture to the quince juice and stir well.

- Add the remaining sugar and lemon juice to the pot and bring to a boil over high heat.

- Stir frequently and let the mixture boil for 1 minute.

- Remove from heat and skim any foam from the surface of the jelly.

- Ladle the jelly into sterilized jars, leaving 1/4 inch of headspace.

- Wipe the rims of the jars clean and seal with lids and bands.

- Process in a boiling water canner for 10 minutes.

RED CURRANT JELLY

Ingredients:

- 5 cups of red currants

- 4 cups of granulated sugar

- 1/4 cup of lemon juice

- 1 package of pectin

Directions:

- Wash the red currants and remove any stems or leaves.

- Place the red currants in a large pot and add enough water to cover them.

- Bring the mixture to a boil over high heat and then reduce to a simmer for 15-20 minutes.

- Strain the red currant juice through a fine-mesh sieve or cheesecloth.

- Measure 4 cups of the red currant juice into a pot.

- Mix the pectin with 1/4 cup of sugar in a separate bowl.

- Add the pectin mixture to the red currant juice and stir well.

- Add the remaining sugar and lemon juice to the pot and bring to a boil over high heat.

- Stir frequently and let the mixture boil for 1 minute.

- Remove from heat and skim any foam from the surface of the jelly.

- Ladle the jelly into sterilized jars, leaving 1/4 inch of headspace.

- Wipe the rims of the jars clean and seal with lids and bands.

- Process in a boiling water canner for 10 minutes.

ELDERBERRY JELLY

Ingredients:

- 5 cups of elderberries

- 4 cups of granulated sugar

- 1/4 cup of lemon juice

- 1 package of pectin

Directions:

- Wash the elderberries and remove any stems or leaves.

- Place the elderberries in a large pot and add enough water to cover them.

- Bring the mixture to a boil over high heat and then reduce to a simmer for 15-20 minutes.

- Strain the elderberry juice through a fine-mesh sieve or cheesecloth.

- Measure 4 cups of the elderberry juice into a pot.

- Mix the pectin with 1/4 cup of sugar in a separate bowl.

- Add the pectin mixture to the elderberry juice and stir well.

- Add the remaining sugar and lemon juice to the pot and bring to a boil over high heat.

- Stir frequently and let the mixture boil for 1 minute.

- Remove from heat and skim any foam from the surface of the jelly.

- Ladle the jelly into sterilized jars, leaving 1/4 inch of headspace.

- Wipe the rims of the jars clean and seal with lids and bands.

- Process in a boiling water canner for 10 minutes.

CRAB APPLE JELLY

Ingredients:

- 5 cups of crab apples, chopped
- 4 cups of granulated sugar
- 1/4 cup of lemon juice
- 1 package of pectin

Directions:

- Wash and chop the crab apples into small pieces, leaving the skin and seeds intact.
- Place the crab apples in a large pot and add enough water to cover them.
- Bring the mixture to a boil over high heat and then reduce to a simmer for 20-25 minutes.
- Strain the crab apple juice through a fine-mesh sieve or cheesecloth.
- Measure 4 cups of the crab apple juice into a pot.
- Mix the pectin with 1/4 cup of sugar in a separate bowl.
- Add the pectin mixture to the crab apple juice and stir well.
- Add the remaining sugar and lemon juice to the pot and bring to a boil over high heat.
- Stir frequently and let the mixture boil for 1 minute.
- Remove from heat and skim any foam from the surface of the jelly.
- Ladle the jelly into sterilized jars, leaving 1/4 inch of headspace.
- Wipe the rims of the jars clean and seal with lids and bands.
- Process in a boiling water canner for 10 minutes.

CHERRY JAM

Ingredients:

- 5 cups of cherries, pitted and chopped
- 4 cups of granulated sugar
- 1/4 cup of lemon juice

- 1 package of pectin

Directions:

- Wash and pit the cherries, then chop them into small pieces.
- Place the cherries in a large pot and add enough water to cover them.
- Bring the mixture to a boil over high heat and then reduce to a simmer for 20-25 minutes.
- Strain the cherry juice through a fine-mesh sieve or cheesecloth.
- Measure 4 cups of the cherry juice into a pot.
- Mix the pectin with 1/4 cup of sugar in a separate bowl.
- Add the pectin mixture to the cherry juice and stir well.
- Add the remaining sugar and lemon juice to the pot and bring to a boil over high heat.
- Stir frequently and let the mixture boil for 1 minute.
- Remove from heat and skim any foam from the surface of the jam.
- Ladle the jam into sterilized jars, leaving 1/4 inch of headspace.
- Wipe the rims of the jars clean and seal with lids and bands.
- Process in a boiling water canner for 10 minutes.

ORANGE MARMALADE

Ingredients:

- 4 large oranges
- 1 lemon
- 8 cups of water
- 8 cups of granulated sugar
- 1 package of pectin

Directions:

- Wash the oranges and lemon and cut into thin slices, removing any seeds.
- Place the fruit slices in a large pot and add enough water to cover them.

- Bring the mixture to a boil over high heat and then reduce to a simmer for 1-2 hours until the fruit is soft and the liquid has reduced.
- Measure the cooked fruit and liquid and add enough water to make 8 cups.
- Mix the pectin with 1/4 cup of sugar in a separate bowl.
- Add the fruit mixture to a pot and stir in the pectin mixture.
- Bring to a boil over high heat, stirring frequently.
- Add the remaining sugar and continue boiling for 1 minute, stirring constantly.
- Remove from heat and skim any foam from the surface of the marmalade.
- Ladle the marmalade into sterilized jars, leaving 1/4 inch of headspace.
- Wipe the rims of the jars clean and seal with lids and bands.
- Process in a boiling water canner for 10 minutes.

FIG JAM

Ingredients:

- 5 cups of fresh figs, chopped
- 4 cups of granulated sugar
- 1/4 cup of lemon juice
- 1 package of pectin

Directions:

- Wash and chop the figs into small pieces.
- Place the figs in a large pot and add enough water to cover them.
- Bring the mixture to a boil over high heat and then reduce to a simmer for 20-25 minutes.
- Strain the fig juice through a fine-mesh sieve or cheesecloth.
- Measure 4 cups of the fig juice into a pot.
- Mix the pectin with 1/4 cup of sugar in a separate bowl.
- Add the pectin mixture to the fig juice and stir well.
- Add the remaining sugar and lemon juice to the pot and bring to a boil over high
- Stir frequently and let the mixture boil for 1 minute.

- Remove from heat and skim any foam from the surface of the jam.
- Ladle the jam into sterilized jars, leaving 1/4 inch of headspace.
- Wipe the rims of the jars clean and seal with lids and bands.
- Process in a boiling water canner for 10 minutes.

APRICOT JAM

Ingredients:

- 5 cups of fresh apricots, pitted and chopped
- 4 cups of granulated sugar
- 1/4 cup of lemon juice
- 1 package of pectin

Directions:

- Wash and pit the apricots, then chop them into small pieces.
- Place the apricots in a large pot and add enough water to cover them.
- Bring the mixture to a boil over high heat and then reduce to a simmer for 20-25 minutes.
- Strain the apricot juice through a fine-mesh sieve or cheesecloth.
- Measure 4 cups of the apricot juice into a pot.
- Mix the pectin with 1/4 cup of sugar in a separate bowl.
- Add the pectin mixture to the apricot juice and stir well.
- Add the remaining sugar and lemon juice to the pot and bring to a boil over high heat.
- Stir frequently and let the mixture boil for 1 minute.
- Remove from heat and skim any foam from the surface of the jam.
- Ladle the jam into sterilized jars, leaving 1/4 inch of headspace.
- Wipe the rims of the jars clean and seal with lids and bands.
- Process in a boiling water canner for 10 minutes.

MIXED FRUIT JAM

Ingredients:

- 2 cups of strawberries, hulled and chopped
- 2 cups of blueberries
- 2 cups of raspberries
- 2 cups of blackberries
- 7 cups of granulated sugar
- 1/4 cup of lemon juice
- 1 package of pectin

Directions:

- Wash and chop the strawberries and mix them with the blueberries, raspberries, and blackberries.
- Place the fruit mixture in a large pot and add enough water to cover them.
- Bring the mixture to a boil over high heat and then reduce to a simmer for 20-25 minutes.
- Strain the mixed fruit juice through a fine-mesh sieve or cheesecloth.
- Measure 4 cups of the mixed fruit juice into a pot.
- Mix the pectin with 1/4 cup of sugar in a separate bowl.
- Add the pectin mixture to the mixed fruit juice and stir well.
- Add the remaining sugar and lemon juice to the pot and bring to a boil over high heat.
- Stir frequently and let the mixture boil for 1 minute.
- Remove from heat and skim any foam from the surface of the jam.
- Ladle the jam into sterilized jars, leaving 1/4 inch of headspace.
- Wipe the rims of the jars clean and seal with lids and bands.
- Process in a boiling water canner for 10 minutes.

MULBERRY JAM

Ingredients:

- 5 cups of fresh mulberries
- 4 cups of granulated sugar

- 1/4 cup of lemon juice
- 1 package of pectin

Directions:

- Wash the mulberries and remove any stems.
- Place the mulberries in a large pot and add enough water to cover them.
- Bring the mixture to a boil over high heat and then reduce to a simmer for 20-25 minutes.
- 4. Strain the mulberry juice through a fine-mesh sieve or cheesecloth.
- Measure 4 cups of the mulberry juice into a pot.
- Mix the pectin with 1/4 cup of sugar in a separate bowl.
- Add the pectin mixture to the mulberry juice and stir well.
- Add the remaining sugar and lemon juice to the pot and bring to a boil over high heat.
- Stir frequently and let the mixture boil for 1 minute.
- Remove from heat and skim any foam from the surface of the jam.
- Ladle the jam into sterilized jars, leaving 1/4 inch of headspace.
- Wipe the rims of the jars clean and seal with lids and bands.
- Process in a boiling water canner for 10 minutes.

GOOSEBERRY JAM

Ingredients:

- 5 cups of fresh gooseberries, washed and stemmed
- 4 cups of granulated sugar
- 1/4 cup of lemon juice
- 1 package of pectin

Directions:

- Wash the gooseberries and remove any stems.
- Place the gooseberries in a large pot and add enough water to cover them.
- Bring the mixture to a boil over high heat and then reduce to a simmer for 20-25 minutes.

- Strain the gooseberry juice through a fine-mesh sieve or cheesecloth.

- Measure 4 cups of the gooseberry juice into a pot.

- Mix the pectin with 1/4 cup of sugar in a separate bowl.

- Add the pectin mixture to the gooseberry juice and stir well.

- Add the remaining sugar and lemon juice to the pot and bring to a boil over high heat.

- Stir frequently and let the mixture boil for 1 minute.

- Remove from heat and skim any foam from the surface of the jam.

- Ladle the jam into sterilized jars, leaving 1/4 inch of headspace.

- Wipe the rims of the jars clean and seal with lids and bands.

- Process in a boiling water canner for 10 minutes.

KIWI JAM

Ingredients:

- 4 cups of peeled and mashed kiwi fruit

- 4 cups of granulated sugar

- 1/4 cup of lemon juice

- 1 package of pectin

Directions:

- Peel and mash the kiwi fruit until it is smooth.

- Place the mashed kiwi in a large pot and add enough water to cover it.

- Bring the mixture to a boil over high heat and then reduce to a simmer for 20-25 minutes.

- Measure 4 cups of the kiwi juice into a pot.

- Mix the pectin with 1/4 cup of sugar in a separate bowl.

- Add the pectin mixture to the kiwi juice and stir well.

- Add the remaining sugar and lemon juice to the pot and bring to a boil over high heat.

- Stir frequently and let the mixture boil for 1 minute.

- Remove from heat and skim any foam from the surface of the jam.

- Ladle the jam into sterilized jars, leaving 1/4 inch of headspace.

- Wipe the rims of the jars clean and seal with lids and bands.
- Process in a boiling water canner for 10 minutes.

Note: Please, it is important to follow canning and preserving guidelines for safe and successful preservation of these recipes.

Pickling Recipes:

BREAD AND BUTTER PICKLES:

Ingredients:

- 8 cups thinly sliced cucumbers
- 2 cups thinly sliced onions
- 1/4 cup pickling salt
- 1 1/2 cups white vinegar
- 1 1/2 cups granulated sugar
- 2 tablespoons mustard seeds
- 1 tablespoon celery seeds
- 1 tablespoon ground turmeric

Instructions:

- In a large bowl, combine the cucumbers, onions, and pickling salt. Let stand for 2 hours.
- Drain the cucumber mixture and rinse thoroughly with cold water.
- In a large saucepan, combine the vinegar, sugar, mustard seeds, celery seeds, and turmeric. Bring to a boil.
- Add the cucumber mixture to the saucepan and return to a boil.
- Ladle the hot pickle mixture into sterilized jars, leaving 1/4 inch of headspace.
- Process in a boiling water canner for 10 minutes.

DILL PICKLES:

Ingredients:

- 4 cups sliced pickling cucumbers
- 4 cloves garlic, peeled and sliced
- 4 sprigs fresh dill
- 1 tablespoon pickling salt
- 1/2 cup white vinegar
- 2 cups water

Instructions:

- Pack the sliced cucumbers, garlic, and dill into sterilized jars, leaving 1/4 inch of headspace.
- In a large saucepan, combine the pickling salt, vinegar, and water. Bring to a boil.
- Pour the hot pickling liquid over the cucumbers in the jars, leaving 1/4 inch of headspace.
- Seal the jars with sterilized lids and rings.
- Process in a boiling water canner for 10 minutes.

SWEET PICKLES:

Ingredients:

- 6 cups sliced pickling cucumbers
- 2 cups white vinegar
- 2 cups granulated sugar
- 1 tablespoon pickling salt
- 1 tablespoon mustard seeds
- 1 tablespoon celery seeds

Instructions:

- In a large saucepan, combine the vinegar, sugar, pickling salt, mustard seeds, and celery seeds. Bring to a boil.

- Add the sliced cucumbers to the saucepan and return to a boil.

- Ladle the hot pickle mixture into sterilized jars, leaving 1/4 inch of headspace.

- Process in a boiling water canner for 10 minutes.

PICKLED BEETS:

Ingredients:

- 6 cups sliced cooked beets

- 2 cups white vinegar

- 1 cup granulated sugar

- 1 tablespoon pickling salt

- 1 cinnamon stick

- 6 whole cloves

Instructions:

- In a large saucepan, combine the vinegar, sugar, pickling salt, cinnamon stick, and cloves. Bring to a boil.

- Add the sliced beets to the saucepan and return to a boil.

- Ladle the hot pickle mixture into sterilized jars, leaving 1/4 inch of headspace.

- Process in a boiling water canner for 10 minutes.

PICKLED CARROTS:

Ingredients:

- 6 cups sliced carrots

- 2 cups white vinegar

- 1 cup granulated sugar

- 1 tablespoon pickling salt

- 2 teaspoons mustard seeds

- 1 teaspoon celery seeds

Instructions:

- In a large saucepan, combine the vinegar, sugar, pickling salt, mustard seeds, and celery seeds. Bring to a boil.
- Add the sliced carrots to the saucepan and return to a boil.
- Ladle the hot pickle mixture into sterilized jars, leaving 1/4 inch of headspace.
- Process in a boiling water canner for 10 minutes.

PICKLED CUCUMBERS:

Ingredients:

- 6 cups sliced pickling cucumbers
- 2 cups white vinegar
- 1 cup granulated sugar
- 1 tablespoon pickling salt
- 1 tablespoon mustard seeds
- 1 tablespoon celery seeds

Instructions:

- In a large saucepan, combine the vinegar, sugar, pickling salt, mustard seeds, and celery seeds. Bring to a boil.
- Add the sliced cucumbers to the saucepan and return to a boil.
- Ladle the hot pickle mixture into sterilized jars, leaving 1/4 inch of headspace.
- Process in a boiling water canner for 10 minutes.

PICKLED OKRA:

Ingredients:

- 4 cups sliced okra pods

- 1 cup white vinegar
- 1 cup water
- 2 cloves garlic, peeled
- 2 teaspoons pickling salt
- 1 teaspoon dill seeds

Instructions:

- In a large saucepan, combine the vinegar, water, garlic cloves, pickling salt, and dill seeds. Bring to a boil.
- Pack the sliced okra pods into sterilized jars, leaving 1/4 inch of headspace.
- Pour the hot pickle mixture over the okra in the jars, leaving 1/4 inch of headspace.
- Seal the jars with sterilized lids and rings.
- Process in a boiling water canner for 10 minutes.

PICKLED PEPPERS:

Ingredients:

- 4 cups sliced peppers (use a mix of hot and sweet peppers)
- 1 1/2 cups white vinegar
- 1 1/2 cups water
- 1 tablespoon pickling salt
- 1 tablespoon sugar

Instructions:

- In a large saucepan, combine the vinegar, water, pickling salt, and sugar. Bring to a boil.
- Pack the sliced peppers into sterilized jars, leaving 1/4 inch of headspace.
- Pour the hot pickle mixture over the peppers in the jars, leaving 1/4 inch of headspace.
- Seal the jars with sterilized lids and rings.
- Process in a boiling water canner for 10 minutes.

PICKLED RADISHES:

Ingredients:

- 4 cups sliced radishes
- 1 cup white vinegar
- 1 cup water
- 1 tablespoon pickling salt
- 2 cloves garlic, peeled
- 1 teaspoon mustard seeds

Instructions:

- In a large saucepan, combine the vinegar, water, pickling salt, garlic cloves, and mustard seeds. Bring to a boil.
- Pack the sliced radishes into sterilized jars, leaving 1/4 inch of headspace.
- Pour the hot pickle mixture over the radishes in the jars, leaving 1/4 inch of headspace.
- Seal the jars with sterilized lids and rings.
- Process in a boiling water canner for 10 minutes.

PICKLED TURNIPS:

Ingredients:

- 4 cups sliced turnips
- 1 cup white vinegar
- 1 cup water
- 1 tablespoon pickling salt
- 2 cloves garlic, peeled
- 1 teaspoon coriander seeds

Instructions:

- In a large saucepan, combine the vinegar, water, pickling salt, garlic cloves, and coriander seeds. Bring to a boil.

- Pack the sliced turnips into sterilized jars, leaving 1/4 inch of head space.
- Pour the hot pickle mixture over the turnips in the jars, leaving 1/4 inch of headspace.
- Seal the jars with sterilized lids and rings.
- Process in a boiling water canner for 10 minutes.

PICKLED ONIONS:

Ingredients:

- 4 cups sliced onions
- 1 1/2 cups white vinegar
- 1 1/2 cups water
- 1 tablespoon pickling salt
- 2 cloves garlic, peeled
- 1 teaspoon black peppercorns

Instructions:

- In a large saucepan, combine the vinegar, water, pickling salt, garlic cloves, and black peppercorns. Bring to a boil.
- Pack the sliced onions into sterilized jars, leaving 1/4 inch of headspace.
- Pour the hot pickle mixture over the onions in the jars, leaving 1/4 inch of headspace.
- Seal the jars with sterilized lids and rings.
- Process in a boiling water canner for 10 minutes.

PICKLED GARLIC:

Ingredients:

- 2 cups peeled garlic cloves
- 1 1/2 cups white vinegar
- 1 1/2 cups water

- 1 tablespoon pickling salt
- 2 teaspoons mustard seeds
- 2 teaspoons dill seeds

Instructions:

- In a large saucepan, combine the vinegar, water, pickling salt, mustard seeds, and dill seeds. Bring to a boil.
- Pack the peeled garlic cloves into sterilized jars, leaving 1/4 inch of headspace.
- Pour the hot pickle mixture over the garlic cloves in the jars, leaving 1/4 inch of headspace.
- Seal the jars with sterilized lids and rings.
- Process in a boiling water canner for 10 minutes.

PICKLED GREEN TOMATOES:

Ingredients:

- 4 cups sliced green tomatoes
- 1 1/2 cups white vinegar
- 1 1/2 cups water
- 1 tablespoon pickling salt
- 1 tablespoon sugar
- 1 teaspoon mustard seeds

Instructions:

- In a large saucepan, combine the vinegar, water, pickling salt, sugar, and mustard seeds. Bring to a boil.
- Pack the sliced green tomatoes into sterilized jars, leaving 1/4 inch of headspace.
- Pour the hot pickle mixture over the green tomatoes in the jars, leaving 1/4 inch of headspace.
- Seal the jars with sterilized lids and rings.
- Process in a boiling water canner for 10 minutes.

PICKLED WATERMELON RIND:

Ingredients:

- 6 cups peeled and sliced watermelon rind
- 2 cups white vinegar
- 1 cup water
- 1 cinnamon stick
- 1 tablespoon pickling salt
- 1 tablespoon whole cloves
- 1 tablespoon whole allspice

Instructions:

- In a large saucepan, combine the vinegar, water, cinnamon stick, pickling salt, whole cloves, and whole allspice. Bring to a boil.
- Add the sliced watermelon rind to the saucepan and return to a boil.
- Ladle the hot pickle mixture into sterilized jars, leaving 1/4 inch of headspace.
- Process in a boiling water canner for 10 minutes.

PICKLED CORN:

Ingredients:

- 4 cups cooked corn kernels
- 1 cup white vinegar
- 1 cup water
- 1 tablespoon pickling salt
- 1 teaspoon cumin seeds
- 1 teaspoon coriander seeds

Instructions:

- In a large saucepan, combine the vinegar, water, pickling salt, cumin seeds, and coriander seeds. Bring to a boil.

- Pack the cooked corn kernels into sterilized jars, leaving 1/4 inch of headspace.
- Pour the hot pickle mixture over the corn kernels in the jars, leaving 1/4 inch of headspace.
- Seal the jars with sterilized lids and rings.
- Process in a boiling water canner for 10 minutes.

PICKLED ASPARAGUS:

Ingredients:

- 2 pounds asparagus, trimmed to fit into jars
- 3 cups white vinegar
- 3 cups water
- 3 tablespoons pickling salt
- 2 teaspoons mustard seeds
- 2 teaspoons dill seeds
- 2 cloves garlic, peeled

Instructions:

- In a large saucepan, combine the vinegar, water, pickling salt, mustard seeds, dill seeds, and garlic cloves. Bring to a boil.
- Pack the trimmed asparagus spears into sterilized jars, leaving 1/4 inch of headspace.
- Pour the hot pickle mixture over the asparagus spears in the jars, leaving 1/4 inch of headspace.
- Seal the jars with sterilized lids and rings.
- Process in a boiling water canner for 10 minutes.

PICKLED GINGER:

Ingredients:

- 1 pound fresh ginger root, peeled and sliced
- 2 cups rice vinegar

- 1 cup water
- 1/2 cup sugar
- 1 tablespoon pickling salt

Instructions:

- In a large saucepan, combine the rice vinegar, water, sugar, and pickling salt. Bring to a boil.
- Pack the sliced ginger into sterilized jars, leaving 1/4 inch of headspace.
- Pour the hot pickle mixture over the ginger in the jars, leaving 1/4 inch of headspace.
- Seal the jars with sterilized lids and rings.
- Process in a boiling water canner for 10 minutes.

PICKLED CAULIFLOWER:

Ingredients:

- 2 heads cauliflower, broken into florets
- 2 cups white vinegar
- 2 cups water
- 1 tablespoon pickling salt
- 1 teaspoon mustard seeds
- 1 teaspoon coriander seeds
- 1 teaspoon dill seeds

Instructions:

- In a large saucepan, combine the white vinegar, water, pickling salt, mustard seeds, coriander seeds, and dill seeds. Bring to a boil.
- Pack the cauliflower florets into sterilized jars, leaving 1/4 inch of headspace.
- Pour the hot pickle mixture over the cauliflower florets in the jars, leaving 1/4 inch of headspace.
- Seal the jars with sterilized lids and rings.
- Process in a boiling water canner for 10 minutes.

PICKLED BRUSSEL SPROUTS:

Ingredients:

- 2 pounds Brussel sprouts, trimmed and halved
- 3 cups white vinegar
- 3 cups water
- 3 tablespoons pickling salt
- 2 teaspoons mustard seeds
- 2 teaspoons dill seeds
- 2 cloves garlic, peeled

Instructions:

- In a large saucepan, combine the vinegar, water, pickling salt, mustard seeds, dill seeds, and garlic cloves. Bring to a boil.
- Pack the halved Brussel sprouts into sterilized jars, leaving 1/4 inch of headspace.
- Pour the hot pickle mixture over the Brussel sprouts in the jars, leaving 1/4 inch of headspace.
- Seal the jars with sterilized lids and rings.
- Process in a boiling water canner for 10 minutes.

PICKLED EGGS:

Ingredients:

- 1 dozen hard-boiled eggs, peeled
- 2 cups white vinegar
- 2 cups water
- 1/4 cup sugar
- 1 tablespoon pickling salt
- 1 teaspoon mustard seeds
- 1 teaspoon dill seeds
- 1 teaspoon black peppercorns

Instructions:

- In a large saucepan, combine the white vinegar, water, sugar, pickling salt, mustard seeds, dill seeds, and black peppercorns. Bring to a boil.
- Pack the peeled hard-boiled eggs into sterilized jars, leaving 1/4 inch of headspace.
- Pour the hot pickle mixture over the eggs in the jars, leaving 1/4 inch of headspace.
- Seal the jars with sterilized lids and rings.
- Refrigerate the pickled eggs for at least 24 hours before serving. They will keep in the refrigerator for up to two weeks.

Note: These recipes are for water bath canning. If you prefer to use a pressure canner, please consult a reliable source for recommended processing times and pressures. Also, make sure to follow proper safety and sanitation procedures when canning and preserving foods.

Salsas and Chutneys Recipes:

TOMATO SALSA

Ingredients:

- 4 cups chopped tomatoes
- 1/2 cup chopped onion
- 2 garlic cloves, minced
- 2 jalapeño peppers, seeded and minced
- 1/4 cup fresh cilantro, chopped
- 1 tablespoon lime juice
- 1/2 teaspoon salt

Instructions:

- Combine all ingredients in a large pot and bring to a boil.
- Reduce heat and simmer for 10 minutes.
- Ladle hot salsa into hot jars, leaving 1/2 inch headspace.

- Process in a boiling water canner for 15 minutes.
- Let cool and store in a cool, dark place for up to one year.

PINEAPPLE SALSA

Ingredients:

- 2 cups chopped pineapple
- 1/2 cup chopped red onion
- 1 red bell pepper, chopped
- 1/4 cup chopped fresh cilantro
- 1 jalapeño pepper, seeded and minced
- 2 tablespoons lime juice
- 1/2 teaspoon salt
- Instructions:

- Combine all ingredients in a large bowl and mix well.
- Ladle salsa into hot jars, leaving 1/2 inch headspace.
- Process in a boiling water canner for 15 minutes.
- Let cool and store in a cool, dark place for up to one year.

MANGO SALSA

Ingredients:

- 2 cups chopped mango
- 1/2 cup chopped red onion
- 1 red bell pepper, chopped
- 1/4 cup chopped fresh cilantro
- 1 jalapeño pepper, seeded and minced

- 2 tablespoons lime juice
- 1/2 teaspoon salt

Instructions:

- Combine all ingredients in a large bowl and mix well.
- Ladle salsa into hot jars, leaving 1/2 inch headspace.
- Process in a boiling water canner for 15 minutes.
- Let cool and store in a cool, dark place for up to one year.

PEACH SALSA

Ingredients:

- 2 cups chopped peaches
- 1/2 cup chopped red onion
- 1 red bell pepper, chopped
- 1/4 cup chopped fresh cilantro
- 1 jalapeño pepper, seeded and minced
- 2 tablespoons lime juice
- 1/2 teaspoon salt

Instructions:

- Combine all ingredients in a large bowl and mix well.
- Ladle salsa into hot jars, leaving 1/2 inch headspace.
- Process in a boiling water canner for 15 minutes.
- Let cool and store in a cool, dark place for up to one year.

CORN SALSA

Ingredients:

- 2 cups corn kernels

- 1/2 cup chopped red onion
- 1 red bell pepper, chopped
- 1/4 cup chopped fresh cilantro
- 1 jalapeño pepper, seeded and minced
- 2 tablespoons lime juice
- 1/2 teaspoon salt

Instructions:

- Combine all ingredients in a large bowl and mix well.
- Ladle salsa into hot jars, leaving 1/2 inch headspace.
- Process in a boiling water canner for 15 minutes.
- Let cool and store in a cool, dark place for up to one year.

BLACK BEAN SALSA

Ingredients:

- 1 can black beans, drained and rinsed
- 1/2 cup chopped red onion
- 1 red bell pepper, chopped
- 1/4 cup chopped fresh cilantro
- 1 jalapeño pepper, seeded and minced
- 2 tablespoons lime juice
- 1/2 teaspoon salt

Instructions:

- In a large bowl, combine the black beans, red onion, red bell pepper, cilantro, jalapeño pepper, lime juice, and salt.
- Mix well.
- Ladle salsa into hot jars, leaving 1/2 inch headspace.
- Process in a boiling water canner for 15 minutes.

- Let cool and store in a cool, dark place for up to one year.

AVOCADO SALSA

Ingredients:

- 2 ripe avocados, diced
- 1/2 cup chopped red onion
- 1 red bell pepper, chopped
- 1/4 cup chopped fresh cilantro
- 1 jalapeño pepper, seeded and minced
- 2 tablespoons lime juice
- 1/2 teaspoon salt

Instructions:

- In a large bowl, gently mix together the diced avocados, red onion, red bell pepper, cilantro, jalapeño pepper, lime juice, and salt.
- Ladle salsa into hot jars, leaving 1/2 inch headspace.
- Process in a boiling water canner for 15 minutes.
- Let cool and store in a cool, dark place for up to one year.

CRANBERRY CHUTNEY

Ingredients:

- 1 pound fresh cranberries
- 1 cup brown sugar
- 1 cup chopped onion
- 1/2 cup chopped apple
- 1/2 cup raisins
- 1/2 cup apple cider vinegar

- 1 teaspoon ground cinnamon
- 1/2 teaspoon ground ginger
- 1/4 teaspoon ground cloves

Instructions:

- In a large pot, combine the cranberries, brown sugar, onion, apple, raisins, apple cider vinegar, cinnamon, ginger, and cloves.
- Bring the mixture to a boil, then reduce heat and simmer for 30 minutes, stirring occasionally.
- Ladle chutney into hot jars, leaving 1/2 inch headspace.
- Process in a boiling water canner for 15 minutes.
- Let cool and store in a cool, dark place for up to one year.

PEACH CHUTNEY

Ingredients:

- 4 cups chopped peaches
- 1 cup brown sugar
- 1/2 cup chopped onion
- 1/2 cup raisins
- 1/2 cup apple cider vinegar
- 1/2 teaspoon ground ginger
- 1/4 teaspoon ground cloves

Instructions:

- In a large pot, combine the peaches, brown sugar, onion, raisins, apple cider vinegar, ginger, and cloves.
- Bring the mixture to a boil, then reduce heat and simmer for 30 minutes, stirring occasionally.
- Ladle chutney into hot jars, leaving 1/2 inch headspace.
- Process in a boiling water canner for 15 minutes.
- Let cool and store in a cool, dark place for up to one year.

APPLE CHUTNEY

Ingredients:

- 4 cups chopped apples
- 1 cup brown sugar
- 1/2 cup chopped onion
- 1/2 cup raisins
- 1/2 cup apple cider vinegar
- 1 teaspoon ground cinnamon
- 1/2 teaspoon ground ginger
- 1/4 teaspoon ground cloves

Instructions:

- In a large pot, combine the apples, brown sugar, onion, raisins, apple cider vinegar, cinnamon, ginger, and cloves.
- Bring the mixture to a boil, then reduce heat and simmer for 30 minutes, stirring occasionally.
- Ladle chutney into hot jars, leaving 1/2 inch headspace.
- Process in a boiling water canner for 15 minutes.
- Let cool and store in a cool, dark place for up to one year.

MANGO CHUTNEY

Ingredients:

- 4 cups chopped mangoes
- 1 cup brown sugar
- 1/2 cup chopped onion
- 1/2 cup raisins
- 1/2 cup apple cider vinegar
- 1 teaspoon ground ginger

- 1/4 teaspoon ground cloves

Instructions:

- In a large pot, combine the mangoes, brown sugar, onion, raisins, apple cider vinegar, ginger, and cloves.
- Bring the mixture to a boil, then reduce heat and simmer for 30 minutes, stirring occasionally.
- Ladle chutney into hot jars, leaving 1/2 inch headspace.
- Process in a boiling water canner for 15 minutes.
- Let cool and store in a cool, dark place for up to one year.

TOMATO CHUTNEY

Ingredients:

- 4 cups chopped tomatoes
- 1 cup brown sugar
- 1/2 cup chopped onion
- 1/2 cup raisins
- 1/2 cup apple cider vinegar
- 1 teaspoon ground cinnamon
- 1/2 teaspoon ground ginger
- 1/4 teaspoon ground cloves

Instructions:

- In a large pot, combine the tomatoes, brown sugar, onion, raisins, apple cider vinegar, cinnamon, ginger, and cloves.
- Bring the mixture to a boil, then reduce heat and simmer for 30 minutes, stirring occasionally.
- Ladle chutney into hot jars, leaving 1/2 inch headspace.
- Process in a boiling water canner for 15 minutes.
- Let cool and store in a cool, dark place for up to one year.

ONION CHUTNEY

Ingredients:

- 4 cups chopped onions
- 1 cup brown sugar
- 1/2 cup apple cider vinegar
- 1/2 teaspoon ground cinnamon
- 1/2 teaspoon ground ginger
- 1/4 teaspoon ground cloves

Instructions:

- In a large pot, combine the onions, brown sugar, apple cider vinegar, cinnamon, ginger, and cloves.
- Bring the mixture to a boil, then reduce heat and simmer for 30 minutes, stirring occasionally.
- Ladle chutney into hot jars, leaving 1/2 inch headspace.
- Process in a boiling water canner for 15 minutes.
- Let cool and store in a cool, dark place for up to one year.

TAMARIND CHUTNEY

Ingredients:

- 1 cup tamarind paste
- 1 cup brown sugar
- 1/2 cup chopped dates
- 1/2 cup apple cider vinegar
- 1 teaspoon ground ginger
- 1/4 teaspoon ground cloves

Instructions:

- In a large pot, combine the tamarind paste, brown sugar, dates, apple cider vinegar, ginger, and cloves.
- Bring the mixture to a boil, then reduce heat and simmer for 30 minutes, stirring occasionally.

- Ladle chutney into hot jars, leaving 1/2 inch headspace.
- Process in a boiling water canner for 15 minutes.
- Let cool and store in a cool, dark place for up to one year.

MINT CHUTNEY

Ingredients:

- 2 cups fresh mint leaves
- 1/2 cup chopped onion
- 1/4 cup chopped jalapeño pepper
- 1/4 cup lemon juice
- 1 teaspoon salt

Instructions:

- In a food processor, combine the mint leaves, onion, jalapeño pepper, lemon juice, and salt.
- Pulse until the mixture is finely chopped.
- Ladle chutney into hot jars, leaving 1/2 inch headspace.
- Process in a boiling water canner for 15 minutes.
- Let cool and store in a cool, dark place for up to one year.

CILANTRO CHUTNEY

Ingredients:

- 2 cups fresh cilantro leaves
- 1/2 cup chopped onion
- 1/4 cup chopped jalapeño pepper
- 1/4 cup lemon juice
- 1 teaspoon salt

Instructions:

- In a food processor, combine the cilantro leaves, onion, jalapeño pepper, lemon juice, and salt.

- Pulse until the mixture is finely chopped.

- Ladle chutney into hot jars, leaving 1/2 inch headspace.

- Process in a boiling water canner for 15 minutes.

- Let cool and store in a cool, dark place for up to one year.

GINGER CHUTNEY

Ingredients:

- 1 cup grated fresh ginger

- 1 cup brown sugar

- 1/2 cup apple cider vinegar

- 1/4 cup lemon juice

- 1/4 teaspoon ground cloves

Instructions:

- In a large pot, combine the grated ginger, brown sugar, apple cider vinegar, lemon juice, and cloves.

- Bring the mixture to a boil, then reduce heat and simmer for 30 minutes, stirring occasionally.

- Ladle chutney into hot jars, leaving 1/2 inch headspace.

- Process in a boiling water canner for 15 minutes.

- Let cool and store in a cool, dark place for up to one year.

CARROT CHUTNEY

Ingredients:

- 4 cups grated carrots

- 1 cup brown sugar

- 1/2 cup apple cider vinegar

- 1/2 teaspoon ground cinnamon

- 1/4 teaspoon ground cloves

Instructions:

- In a large pot, combine the grated carrots, brown sugar, apple cider vinegar, cinnamon, and cloves.
- Bring the mixture to a boil, then reduce heat and simmer for 30 minutes, stirring occasionally.
- Ladle chutney into hot jars, leaving 1/2 inch headspace.
- Process in a boiling water canner for 15 minutes.
- Let cool and store in a cool, dark place for up to one year.

BELL PEPPER CHUTNEY

Ingredients:

- 2 cups chopped bell peppers (a mix of red, yellow, and green)
- 1/2 cup chopped onion
- 1/4 cup chopped jalapeño pepper
- 1/2 cup apple cider vinegar
- 1 teaspoon ground cumin
- 1/4 teaspoon ground cloves

Instructions:

- In a large pot, combine the chopped bell peppers, onion, jalapeño pepper, apple cider vinegar, cumin, and cloves.
- Bring the mixture to a boil, then reduce heat and simmer for 30 minutes, stirring occasionally.
- Ladle chutney into hot jars, leaving 1/2 inch headspace.
- Process in a boiling water canner for 15 minutes.
- Let cool and store in a cool, dark place for up to one year.

Sauces and Syrups Recipes:

TOMATO SAUCE

Ingredients:

- 5 pounds of fresh tomatoes
- 1 large onion, diced
- 4 cloves of garlic, minced
- 1/4 cup of olive oil
- 1 tablespoon of salt
- 1 tablespoon of sugar
- 1 tablespoon of dried basil
- 1 tablespoon of dried oregano
- 1 teaspoon of black pepper

Instructions:

- Wash and chop the tomatoes into small pieces.
- In a large pot, heat the olive oil over medium heat.
- Add the diced onion and minced garlic to the pot and sauté for 5 minutes, or until the onion is translucent.
- Add the chopped tomatoes to the pot and stir well.
- Add the salt, sugar, dried basil, dried oregano, and black pepper to the pot and stir well.
- Bring the mixture to a boil, then reduce the heat and let it simmer for 45-60 minutes, or until the sauce has thickened.
- Using an immersion blender, blend the sauce until it reaches your desired consistency.
- Pour the hot tomato sauce into sterilized canning jars, leaving 1/2 inch of headspace.
- Process the jars in a boiling water bath for 35 minutes.
- Remove the jars from the water bath and let them cool completely before storing in a cool, dark place.

APPLESAUCE

Ingredients:

- 8 cups of peeled, cored, and chopped apples
- 1 cup of water
- 1/2 cup of granulated sugar
- 1/2 teaspoon of ground cinnamon
- 1/4 teaspoon of ground nutmeg
- 1/4 teaspoon of salt

Instructions:

- In a large pot, combine the chopped apples, water, sugar, cinnamon, nutmeg, and salt.
- Bring the mixture to a boil over medium heat, then reduce the heat and let it simmer for 20-25 minutes, or until the apples are soft.
- Using an immersion blender, blend the applesauce until it reaches your desired consistency.
- Pour the hot applesauce into sterilized canning jars, leaving 1/2 inch of headspace.
- Process the jars in a boiling water bath for 15 minutes.
- Remove the jars from the water bath and let them cool completely before storing in a cool, dark place.

PEACH SAUCE

Ingredients:

- 8 cups of peeled, pitted, and chopped peaches
- 1 cup of water
- 1/2 cup of granulated sugar
- 1/2 teaspoon of ground cinnamon
- 1/4 teaspoon of ground nutmeg
- 1/4 teaspoon of salt

Instructions:

- In a large pot, combine the chopped peaches, water, sugar, cinnamon, nutmeg, and salt.
- Bring the mixture to a boil over medium heat, then reduce the heat and let it simmer for 20-25 minutes, or until the peaches are soft.

- Using an immersion blender, blend the peach sauce until it reaches your desired consistency.
- Pour the hot peach sauce into sterilized canning jars, leaving 1/2 inch of headspace.
- Process the jars in a boiling water bath for 15 minutes.
- Remove the jars from the water bath and let them cool completely before storing in a cool, dark place.

BARBECUE SAUCE

Ingredients:

- 2 cups of ketchup
- 1 cup of apple cider vinegar
- 1/2 cup of brown sugar
- 1/2 cup of molasses
- 2 tablespoons of Worcestershire sauce
- 2 tablespoons of Dijon mustard
- 1 tablespoon of smoked paprika
- 1 teaspoon of garlic powder
- 1/2 teaspoon of cayenne pepper (optional)

Instructions:

- In a large saucepan, combine all of the ingredients and stir well.
- Bring the mixture to a boil over medium heat, stirring occasionally.
- Reduce the heat and let the sauce simmer for 10-15 minutes, or until it has thickened to your desired consistency.
- Remove the sauce from the heat and let it cool.
- Pour the cooled barbecue sauce into sterilized canning jars, leaving 1/2 inch of headspace.
- Process the jars in a boiling water bath for 15 minutes.
- Remove the jars from the water bath and let them cool completely before storing in a cool, dark place.

HOT SAUCE

Ingredients:

- 1 pound of hot peppers, such as jalapeños or habaneros
- 2 cups of white vinegar
- 1/2 teaspoon of salt
- 2 garlic cloves, minced

Instructions:

- Wear gloves to handle the hot peppers to avoid burning your skin.
- Remove the stems from the hot peppers and chop them into small pieces.
- In a large saucepan, combine the chopped hot peppers, white vinegar, salt, and minced garlic.
- Bring the mixture to a boil over medium-high heat, then reduce the heat and let it simmer for 10-15 minutes.
- Remove the saucepan from the heat and let the mixture cool for 10-15 minutes.
- Using an immersion blender, blend the hot sauce until it reaches your desired consistency.
- Pour the hot sauce into sterilized canning jars, leaving 1/2 inch of headspace.
- Process the jars in a boiling water bath for 15 minutes.
- Remove the jars from the water bath and let them cool completely before storing in a cool, dark place.

WORCESTERSHIRE SAUCE

Ingredients:

- 2 cups of apple cider vinegar
- 1/2 cup of soy sauce
- 1/4 cup of brown sugar
- 2 tablespoons of molasses
- 1 tablespoon of onion powder
- 1 tablespoon of garlic powder
- 1 tablespoon of ground mustard
- 1/2 teaspoon of ground ginger
- 1/2 teaspoon of black pepper

Instructions:

- In a large saucepan, combine all of the ingredients and stir well.
- Bring the mixture to a boil over medium heat, stirring occasionally.
- Reduce the heat and let the sauce simmer for 30-45 minutes, or until it has thickened to your desired consistency.
- Remove the sauce from the heat and let it cool.
- Pour the cooled Worcestershire sauce into sterilized canning jars, leaving 1/2 inch of headspace.
- Process the jars in a boiling water bath for 15 minutes.
- Remove the jars from the water bath and let them cool completely before storing in a cool, dark place.

MUSTARD SAUCE

Ingredients:

- 1 cup of yellow mustard seeds
- 1 cup of white wine vinegar
- 1/4 cup of honey
- 1/4 cup of brown sugar
- 1 tablespoon of dried thyme
- 1/2 teaspoon of salt
- 1/4 teaspoon of black pepper

Instructions:

- In a large bowl, combine the mustard seeds and white wine vinegar.
- Cover the bowl and let it sit at room temperature for 24 hours.
- After 24 hours, transfer the mustard seed mixture to a blender or food processor.
- Add the honey, brown sugar, dried thyme, salt, and black pepper to the blender or food processor and blend until smooth.
- Pour the mustard sauce into sterilized canning jars, leaving 1/2 inch of headspace.
- Process the jars in a boiling water bath for 15 minutes.
- Remove the jars from the water bath and let them cool completely before storing in a cool, dark place.

CRANBERRY SAUCE

Ingredients:

- 12 ounces of fresh cranberries
- 1 cup of granulated sugar
- 1/2 cup of orange juice
- 1/4 teaspoon of ground cinnamon
- 1/4 teaspoon of ground ginger
- 1/4 teaspoon of ground nutmeg

Instructions:

- In a medium saucepan, combine all of the ingredients and stir well.
- Bring the mixture to a boil over medium-high heat, then reduce the heat and let it simmer for 10-15 minutes.
- Remove the saucepan from the heat and let the cranberry sauce cool to room temperature.
- Pour the cooled cranberry sauce into sterilized canning jars, leaving 1/2 inch of headspace.
- Process the jars in a boiling water bath for 15 minutes.
- Remove the jars from the water bath and let them cool completely before storing in a cool, dark place.

STRAWBERRY SYRUP

Ingredients:

- 2 cups of fresh strawberries, hulled and sliced
- 1 cup of granulated sugar
- 1 cup of water
- 1 tablespoon of lemon juice

Instructions:

- In a medium saucepan, combine the sliced strawberries, sugar, water, and lemon juice.

- Bring the mixture to a boil over medium-high heat, then reduce the heat and let it simmer for 10-15 minutes.
- Remove the saucepan from the heat and let the strawberry syrup cool to room temperature.
- Strain the syrup through a fine mesh sieve into a clean bowl or measuring cup.
- Pour the strawberry syrup into sterilized canning jars, leaving 1/2 inch of headspace.
- Process the jars in a boiling water bath for 10 minutes.
- Remove the jars from the water bath and let them cool completely before storing in a cool, dark place.

BLUEBERRY SYRUP

Ingredients:

- 2 cups of fresh blueberries
- 1 cup of granulated sugar
- 1 cup of water
- 1 tablespoon of lemon juice

Instructions:

- In a medium saucepan, combine the blueberries, sugar, water, and lemon juice.
- Bring the mixture to a boil over medium-high heat, then reduce the heat and let it simmer for 10-15 minutes.
- Remove the saucepan from the heat and let the blueberry syrup cool to room temperature.
- Strain the syrup through a fine mesh sieve into a clean bowl or measuring cup.
- Pour the blueberry syrup into sterilized canning jars, leaving 1/2 inch of headspace.
- Process the jars in a boiling water bath for 10 minutes.
- Remove the jars from the water bath and let them cool completely before storing in a cool, dark place.

RASPBERRY SYRUP

Ingredients:

- 2 cups of fresh raspberries

- 1 cup of granulated sugar
- 1 cup of water
- 1 tablespoon of lemon juice

Instructions:

- In a medium saucepan, combine the raspberries, sugar, water, and lemon juice.
- Bring the mixture to a boil over medium-high heat, then reduce the heat and let it simmer for 10-15 minutes
- Remove the saucepan from the heat and let the raspberry syrup cool to room temperature.
- Strain the syrup through a fine mesh sieve into a clean bowl or measuring cup.
- Pour the raspberry syrup into sterilized canning jars, leaving 1/2 inch of headspace.
- Process the jars in a boiling water bath for 10 minutes.
- Remove the jars from the water bath and let them cool completely before storing in a cool, dark place.

BLACKBERRY SYRUP

Ingredients:

- 2 cups of fresh blackberries
- 1 cup of granulated sugar
- 1 cup of water
- 1 tablespoon of lemon juice

Instructions:

- In a medium saucepan, combine the blackberries, sugar, water, and lemon juice.
- Bring the mixture to a boil over medium-high heat, then reduce the heat and let it simmer for 10-15 minutes.
- Remove the saucepan from the heat and let the blackberry syrup cool to room temperature.
- Strain the syrup through a fine mesh sieve into a clean bowl or measuring cup.
- Pour the blackberry syrup into sterilized canning jars, leaving 1/2 inch of headspace.
- Process the jars in a boiling water bath for 10 minutes.

- Remove the jars from the water bath and let them cool completely before storing in a cool, dark place.

MAPLE SYRUP

Ingredients:

- 2 cups of pure maple syrup
- 1/4 teaspoon of salt

Instructions:

- In a medium saucepan, heat the maple syrup over medium-high heat until it comes to a simmer.
- Add the salt and stir well.
- Let the maple syrup simmer for 10-15 minutes, stirring occasionally.
- Remove the saucepan from the heat and let the maple syrup cool to room temperature.
- Pour the maple syrup into sterilized canning jars, leaving 1/2 inch of headspace.
- Process the jars in a boiling water bath for 10 minutes.
- Remove the jars from the water bath and let them cool completely before storing in a cool, dark place.

HONEY SYRUP

Ingredients:

- 2 cups of honey
- 1/2 cup of water
- 1 tablespoon of lemon juice

Instructions:

- In a medium saucepan, combine the honey, water, and lemon juice.
- Bring the mixture to a boil over medium-high heat, then reduce the heat and let it simmer for 10-15 minutes.
- Remove the saucepan from the heat and let the honey syrup cool to room temperature.
- Pour the honey syrup into sterilized canning jars, leaving 1/2 inch of headspace.

- Process the jars in a boiling water bath for 10 minutes.
- Remove the jars from the water bath and let them cool completely before storing in a cool, dark place.

CHOCOLATE SAUCE

Ingredients:

- 1 cup of heavy cream
- 8 ounces of semisweet chocolate, chopped
- 1/4 cup of granulated sugar
- 2 tablespoons of unsalted butter
- 1/4 teaspoon of salt

Instructions:

- In a medium saucepan, heat the heavy cream over medium-high heat until it comes to a simmer.
- Add the chopped chocolate, sugar, butter, and salt, and stir well.
- Reduce the heat to low and let the chocolate sauce simmer for 5-10 minutes, stirring occasionally.
- Remove the saucepan from the heat and let the chocolate sauce cool to room temperature.
- Pour the chocolate sauce into sterilized canning jars, leaving 1/2 inch of headspace.
- Process the jars in a boiling water bath for 10 minutes.
- Remove the jars from the water bath and let them cool completely before storing in a cool, dark place.

CARAMEL SAUCE

Ingredients:

- 1 cup of granulated sugar
- 1/4 cup of water
- 3/4 cup of heavy cream
- 2 tablespoons of unsalted butter
- 1/2 teaspoon of salt

Instructions:

- In a medium saucepan, combine the sugar and water.
- Cook over medium-high heat, stirring constantly until the sugar dissolves and turns amber in color.
- Remove the saucepan from the heat and add the heavy cream, butter, and salt.
- Return the saucepan to the heat and cook, stirring constantly, until the caramel sauce is smooth and creamy.
- Remove the saucepan from the heat and let the caramel sauce cool to room temperature.
- Pour the caramel sauce into sterilized canning jars, leaving 1/2 inch of headspace.
- Process the jars in a boiling water bath for 10 minutes.
- Remove the jars from the water bath and let them cool completely before storing in a cool, dark place.

BUTTERSCOTCH SAUCE

Ingredients:

- 1 cup of light brown sugar
- 1/2 cup of heavy cream
- 1/2 cup of unsalted butter
- 1/2 teaspoon of salt

Instructions:

- In a medium saucepan, combine the brown sugar, heavy cream, butter, and salt.
- Cook over medium-high heat, stirring constantly until the butterscotch sauce is smooth and creamy.
- Remove the saucepan from the heat and let the butterscotch sauce cool to room temperature.
- Pour the butterscotch sauce into sterilized canning jars, leaving 1/2 inch of headspace.
- Process the jars in a boiling water bath for 10 minutes.
- Remove the jars from the water bath and let them cool completely before storing in a cool, dark place.

STRAWBERRY JAM SAUCE

Ingredients:

- 4 cups of fresh strawberries, hulled and chopped
- 2 cups of granulated sugar
- 1/4 cup of lemon juice
- 1/4 teaspoon of salt

Instructions:

- In a medium saucepan, combine the strawberries, sugar, lemon juice, and salt.
- Cook over medium-high heat, stirring occasionally, until the strawberries have broken down and the mixture has thickened.
- Remove the saucepan from the heat and let the strawberry jam sauce cool to room temperature.
- Pour the strawberry jam sauce into sterilized canning jars, leaving 1/2 inch of headspace.
- Process the jars in a boiling water bath for 10 minutes.
- Remove the jars from the water bath and let them cool completely before storing in a cool, dark place.

CHERRY SAUCE

Ingredients:

- 4 cups of fresh cherries, pitted and chopped
- 1 cup of granulated sugar
- 1/4 cup of water
- 1 tablespoon of lemon juice
- 1/4 teaspoon of salt

Instructions:

- In a medium saucepan, combine the cherries, sugar, water, lemon juice, and salt.
- Cook over medium-high heat, stirring occasionally, until the cherries have broken down and the mixture has thickened.
- Remove the saucepan from the heat and let the cherry sauce cool to room temperature.
- Pour the cherry sauce into sterilized canning jars, leaving 1/2 inch of headspace.
- Process the jars in a boiling water bath for 10 minutes.

- Remove the jars from the water bath and let them cool completely before storing in a cool, dark place.

PEACH SYRUP

Ingredients:

- 4 cups of fresh peaches, peeled and sliced
- 2 cups of granulated sugar
- 1 cup of water

Instructions:

- In a medium saucepan, combine the peaches, sugar, and water.
- Cook over medium-high heat, stirring occasionally, until the peaches have broken down and the mixture has thickened.
- Remove the saucepan from the heat and let the peach syrup cool to room temperature.
- Strain the peach syrup through a fine-mesh strainer into sterilized canning jars, leaving 1/2 inch of headspace.
- Process the jars in a boiling water bath for 10 minutes.
- Remove the jars from the water bath and let them cool completely before storing in a cool, dark place.

CHAPTER 4: AMISH PRESERVING RECIPES

Introduction to Amish Preserving Recipes

In addition to canning, the Amish also have a long tradition of preserving food through techniques such as fermenting, smoking, and drying. These methods not only help to extend the shelf life of fresh fruits and vegetables but also enhance their flavor and nutritional value.

Amish preserving recipes often rely on natural ingredients and traditional techniques to create unique and flavorful foods that can be enjoyed throughout the year. These recipes are typically passed down from generation to generation and reflect the Amish commitment to simple, practical living.

One of the most popular Amish preserving recipes is for sauerkraut, a fermented cabbage dish that is rich in probiotics and other beneficial nutrients. To make sauerkraut, finely shredded cabbage is mixed with salt and packed tightly into a crock or jar. The cabbage is then weighed down with a plate or other heavy object and left to ferment for several days to several weeks. The result is a tangy and flavorful dish that can be used in a variety of recipes.

Another popular Amish preserving recipe is for beef jerky, a dried meat snack that is perfect for on-the-go snacking. To make beef jerky, thinly sliced beef is marinated in a mixture of soy sauce, Worcestershire sauce, garlic, and other seasonings before being dried in a dehydrator or smoker. The result is a chewy and flavorful snack that can be stored for several weeks or even months.

Amish preserving recipes are not limited to sauerkraut and beef jerky, however. Other popular recipes include pickled beets, dried fruits, and smoked meats such as ham and bacon. These recipes reflect the Amish commitment to using natural ingredients and traditional techniques to create delicious and nutritious foods.

It is worth noting that while Amish preserving recipes have been used for generations, it is important to follow modern food safety guidelines to ensure that the food is safely preserved. This includes using clean and sanitized equipment, monitoring fermentation and drying times and temperatures, and storing preserved foods in a cool, dry place.

Drying Foods

Drying foods is a time-honored tradition in many cultures, including the Amish community. It is a method of food preservation that dates back centuries, long before the invention of canning and refrigeration. Drying foods was a necessity for our ancestors, who needed to store food for long periods to sustain themselves through the winter months.

In the Amish community, drying foods is still an important way of preserving the bounty of the harvest. It is a way of preserving the natural flavors and nutrients of fruits, vegetables, and herbs, without the use of artificial preservatives.

The process of drying foods is simple, but it requires patience and attention to detail. First, you need to choose the right foods. Ideally, you want to choose fruits and vegetables that are ripe, but not overripe. Overripe fruits may not dry well, while underripe fruits may not have developed their full flavor. Once you have chosen your fruits and vegetables, it is time to prepare them for drying. This usually involves washing them thoroughly and slicing them into thin, even pieces. You can use a sharp knife or a mandolin slicer to get the slices as even as possible.

Next, you need to arrange the slices on a drying tray. You can use a dehydrator or simply lay the slices out on a baking sheet lined with parchment paper. Make sure the slices are not touching each other, as this can cause them to stick together and not dry properly.

The drying process can take several hours or even days, depending on the food and the drying method. The key is to keep the temperature low and constant, between 120 and 140 degrees Fahrenheit. This allows the food to dry slowly and evenly, without cooking or burning.

Once the food is dry, it should be stored in airtight containers in a cool, dry place. Dried fruits and vegetables can be eaten as a snack or used in cooking and baking. They can also be rehydrated by soaking them in water or other liquids, which brings them back to their original texture and flavor.

Meats are also commonly dried in the Amish community, often using a combination of salt and spices to preserve and flavor the meat. The meat is sliced thinly and placed on drying racks or screens, then seasoned with a mixture of salt, sugar, and spices. The racks are then placed in a cool, dry location for several days until the meat is fully dehydrated and safe to eat.

Herbs are another popular food to dry in the Amish community, as they can be used in a variety of recipes and for medicinal purposes. The herbs are washed and tied into small bundles, then hung upside down in a dry, well-ventilated area until they are fully dehydrated. Once dry, the leaves are removed from the stems and stored in airtight containers for later use.

Drying foods is not just a practical way to preserve food, it is also a way to connect with our ancestors and honor the traditions of the past. By preserving the bounty of the harvest in this way, we can savor the flavors of the season long after it has passed. It is a simple, yet powerful way to celebrate the natural abundance of the earth and the wisdom of those who came before us.

Freezing Foods

Freezing food is a convenient and practical way to preserve fresh produce and meats. The Amish have long used freezing as a means of preserving the bounty of their harvests and ensuring a supply of nourishing food throughout the year. For those who embrace Amish tradition, freezing foods can be a source of joy and satisfaction.

The process of freezing food begins with selecting the right foods. Fresh produce should be harvested at the peak of ripeness and washed thoroughly before being blanched. Blanching involves boiling or steaming the produce for a short period of time to halt the enzymes that cause spoilage and to preserve the color, texture, and nutrients of the food.

After blanching, the food is quickly cooled in ice water to stop the cooking process before being drained and packed into freezer-safe containers. The containers should be labeled with the contents and date before being placed in the freezer.

Meats should be trimmed of excess fat and bone before being wrapped tightly in plastic wrap or freezer paper and labeled with the type of meat and date. For longer-term storage, meats can also be vacuum-sealed.

The joy of freezing food lies not only in the practicality of preserving fresh produce and meats but also in the sense of satisfaction and security that comes with having a well-stocked freezer. The Amish believe in being self-sufficient and taking care of one's own needs, and freezing food is one way to achieve this.

When a well-stocked freezer is combined with other methods of food preservation, such as canning and drying, it can provide a sense of peace and security that comes from being prepared for any eventuality.

In addition to the practical benefits, freezing food can also be an emotionally fulfilling process. There is a sense of pride and accomplishment that comes from growing one's own food, preparing it for storage, and then later enjoying the fruits of one's labor. For the Amish, this process is not just about practicality, but about preserving traditions and values that have been passed down through generations.

In conclusion, freezing is a great way to preserve food in the Amish community. It allows you to enjoy fresh fruits and vegetables throughout the year and is a convenient and easy method of preservation. By following a few simple guidelines, you can ensure that your frozen foods are safe to eat and will retain their flavor and nutrients for months to come. So go ahead, freeze those ripe berries or those extra ears of corn – you'll be glad you did when you're enjoying their fresh taste in the dead of winter.

Fermenting Foods

There is something deeply satisfying about the process of fermenting foods. It is a time-honored tradition that has been passed down through generations, and one that has been embraced by the Amish community as a way of preserving food and promoting good health.

Fermentation is a natural process in which microorganisms, such as bacteria or yeast, break down sugars and produce acids, gases, and alcohols. When it comes to food, fermentation can be used to preserve and enhance the flavor and nutritional value of a wide range of ingredients, from vegetables and fruits to dairy products and meats.

In the Amish community, fermentation is often used to make a variety of foods, including sauerkraut, pickles, kimchi, and kefir. The process is relatively simple and involves just a few key steps.

First, the food to be fermented is washed and chopped into small pieces. For example, in the case of sauerkraut, cabbage is sliced into thin strips. The cabbage is then mixed with salt, which helps to draw out the natural juices and create an environment that is conducive to fermentation.

The mixture is then packed tightly into a clean, sterilized container, such as a crock or a glass jar. It is important to make sure that there is enough liquid to cover the vegetables, as exposure to air can result in spoilage. In some cases, a weight may be placed on top of the vegetables to help keep them submerged.

Next, the container is covered and left at room temperature to ferment. The length of time required for fermentation will depend on the specific recipe and the ambient temperature, but it can range from a few days to several weeks.

During the fermentation process, the bacteria and yeast naturally present on the vegetables begin to break down the sugars and produce lactic acid, which gives fermented foods their characteristic tangy flavor. The acid also acts as a natural preservative, helping to prevent spoilage and extending the shelf life of the food.

Once the fermentation process is complete, the fermented food can be enjoyed immediately, or it can be stored in a cool, dark place for several months. In the case of sauerkraut, for example, it can be canned using traditional water bath canning techniques to ensure that it remains safe to eat for an extended period.

Fermenting foods is a wonderful way to celebrate the natural bounty of the earth and preserve the goodness of fresh ingredients. It is a simple, yet profound, act that connects us to the past and to the wisdom of our ancestors. For the Amish, it is a cherished tradition that honors their commitment to sustainable living and nourishing their bodies and souls with wholesome, homemade food.

Smoking and Curing Meats

Smoking and curing meats is a cherished tradition in the Amish community, and it is a process that has been perfected over generations. It is a labor-intensive process that requires patience and attention to detail, but the results are worth it. The aroma and flavor of smoked and cured meats are simply irresistible, and they are a staple in many Amish homes.

The process of smoking and curing meats begins with selecting the right cut of meat. The Amish prefer to use locally raised animals, such as pigs, cows, and chickens, as they are free from hormones and antibiotics. Once the animal has been slaughtered and dressed, the meat is then cut into the desired portions and prepared for the curing process.

The first step in the curing process is to create a curing mixture, which typically consists of salt, sugar, and various spices. The mixture is then rubbed onto the meat, ensuring that it is evenly distributed. The meat is then placed in a cooler or refrigerator to cure for several days, depending on the size of the cut.

After the meat has been cured, it is time to smoke it. The Amish prefer to use fruitwood or hardwood such as apple, cherry, or hickory, to smoke their meats. The wood is first soaked in water to create smoke, which is then used to flavor and preserve the meat. The meat is then hung on racks or hooks and placed inside a smokehouse. The smokehouse is heated to a low temperature, and the meat is left to smoke for several hours, sometimes even days, depending on the desired level of smokiness.

During the smoking process, the meat develops a rich, smoky flavor and a beautiful color. The smoking process also helps to preserve the meat, allowing it to be stored for long periods without spoiling. Once the meat has been smoked, it is typically hung to air-dry for several days to remove any excess moisture.

The end result of the smoking and curing process is a delicious, flavorful meat that can be enjoyed for months to come. The Amish use these meats in a variety of dishes, including sandwiches, stews, and casseroles. They are also often served as a centerpiece at family gatherings and celebrations.

Making Cheese

Cheese-making is a traditional art that has been practiced by the Amish for generations. It is a skill that requires patience, attention to detail, and a deep understanding of the cheese-making process. In this sub-chapter, we will explore the steps involved in making cheese in the Amish community.

Step 1: Milk Collection

The first step in making cheese is collecting fresh milk. The Amish use milk from their own dairy cows, which are raised on small family farms. The cows are milked twice a day and the milk is collected in stainless steel containers.

Step 2: Coagulation

Once the milk has been collected, it is transferred to a large pot or kettle and heated to a specific temperature. After heating, the milk is then coagulated by adding a starter culture and rennet. The starter culture is a combination of beneficial bacteria that help to acidify the milk and create the desired flavor profile. The rennet is a natural enzyme that causes the milk to coagulate and form curds.

Step 3: Curd Cutting and Stirring

After coagulation, the curd is cut into small pieces using a curd knife. The size of the curd pieces depends on the type of cheese being made. The curd is then stirred to release the whey, which is the liquid portion of the milk.

Step 4: Pressing and Draining

After stirring, the curd is then placed into cheese molds and pressed to remove more whey. The pressing time and pressure depend on the type of cheese being made. The cheese is then removed from the mold and allowed to drain further.

Step 5: Salting and Aging

Once the cheese has been drained, it is then salted to enhance the flavor and promote preservation. The salt can be applied either by rubbing it onto the surface of the cheese or by adding it to the cheese during the curd stirring process. After salting, the cheese is then aged in a temperature and humidity-controlled environment. The length of time the cheese is aged depends on the type of cheese being made and can range from a few weeks to several years.

The Amish community produces a wide variety of cheeses, including cheddar, colby, swiss, and gouda. They also make a unique cheese called "Amish Butter Cheese", which is a semi-soft, buttery cheese that is perfect for snacking or use in recipes.

Making Butter

Oh, the sweet smell of butter in the morning! The Amish community takes pride in their ability to make fresh, delicious butter straight from their dairy cows. It is a process that has been passed down from generation to generation, and one that requires patience, care, and attention to detail. In this sub-chapter, we will explore the process of making butter in the Amish community, and the emotional connection that the Amish have with their butter.

Step 1: Milk Collection

The first step in making butter is collecting fresh milk from the dairy cows. The Amish are known for their small family farms, where the cows are raised with love and care. The milk is collected in stainless steel containers and immediately brought to the kitchen.

Step 2: Separation

Once the milk has been collected, it is left to sit for a period of time to allow the cream to rise to the top. The cream is then carefully skimmed off the top of the milk and placed in a separate container.

Step 3: Churning

The cream is then placed in a churn, which can be either a hand-cranked churn or an electric churn. The churn is then turned until the cream turns into butter. This process can take anywhere from 20 minutes to an hour, depending on the temperature of the cream and the type of churn being used.

Step 4: Washing and Shaping

After the butter has been churned, it is washed with cold water to remove any excess buttermilk. The butter is then shaped into blocks or rolls and wrapped in parchment paper or wax paper for storage.

The Amish community takes great pride in their ability to make fresh, delicious butter. It is a staple in their daily lives, used in everything from cooking to baking. The emotional connection that the Amish have with their butter is one of respect and appreciation for the hard work and dedication that goes into making it. It is a reminder of the simpler times, when things were made by hand with love and care.

CHAPTER 5: AMISH KITCHEN TIPS AND TRICKS

Amish Kitchen Wisdom

The Amish kitchen is a place of warmth, comfort, and simplicity. It is a space where family and community gather to share meals, stories, and laughter. It is a place where the heart of the home beats, and where the spirit of hospitality shines bright. At the heart of Amish kitchen wisdom is the belief that food should nourish both body and soul. This is reflected in their use of fresh, seasonal ingredients, and their commitment to preserving the harvest for the winter months. They believe that food should be simple, yet flavorful, and that meals should be shared with loved ones.

The Amish community has a wealth of culinary knowledge and techniques that have been passed down through generations. These methods of food preparation and preservation have stood the test of time and continue to be used in Amish kitchens today. In this sub-chapter, we will explore some of the key aspects of Amish kitchen wisdom.

One of the foundational principles of Amish kitchen wisdom is the use of natural, wholesome ingredients. The Amish are known for their farming practices, and many grow their own fruits, vegetables, and grains. They believe that the quality of the food we consume directly affects our health, and thus prioritize using fresh, whole ingredients in their cooking.

Another important aspect of Amish kitchen wisdom is the use of time-honored techniques to preserve food. This includes canning, pickling, and fermenting. Canning involves sterilizing jars and filling them with cooked food, such as fruits, vegetables, and meats. Pickling and fermenting involve preserving foods in a brine solution or through the use of beneficial bacteria, respectively. These techniques not only extend the shelf life of food, but also impart unique flavors and textures that cannot be achieved through other methods.

The Amish also value simplicity in their cooking. They believe that food should be nourishing and satisfying without being overly complicated. This means that they often use just a few key ingredients to create dishes that are both flavorful and satisfying. For example, a traditional Amish breakfast might include eggs, bacon, homemade bread, and jam – simple ingredients that come together to create a satisfying meal.

In addition to the techniques and ingredients used in Amish cooking, there is also a strong emphasis on community and sharing. The Amish recognize that food is not just sustenance, but also a means of bringing people together. This is evident in their practice of hosting meals for family and friends, as well as their tradition of community potlucks. They also prioritize helping those in need, often providing meals for families who are going through difficult times.

Finally, the Amish value the importance of hard work and diligence in the kitchen. They understand that preparing food from scratch requires time and effort, but believe that the end result is well worth it. They take pride in their ability to create delicious meals using traditional techniques and simple ingredients, and pass these skills down to future generations.

The Amish community's kitchen wisdom is rooted in a deep respect for natural ingredients, traditional techniques, and community values. By valuing simplicity, hard work, and sharing, the Amish have developed a unique culinary tradition that continues to inspire and delight. Through this cookbook, we hope to share some of these techniques and flavors with you, and inspire you to incorporate Amish kitchen wisdom into your own cooking.

Recipes for Using Canned and Preserved Foods

Preserving food is a way to capture the flavors of summer and enjoy them throughout the year. Whether you are new to canning and preserving or a seasoned expert, it is important to have recipes that make use of your hard work. Here are 15 recipes that celebrate the bounty of the harvest and make use of canned and preserved foods:

- **Canned Tomato Soup**: Nothing beats a comforting bowl of tomato soup on a chilly day. This recipe uses canned tomatoes, along with onions, garlic, and herbs, to create a rich and flavorful soup that will warm you from the inside out.

- **Pickled Red Onion Salad:** This salad is a perfect side dish for any meal. It uses pickled red onions, along with fresh greens and a homemade vinaigrette, to create a tangy and refreshing salad that is both healthy and delicious.

- **Amish Chicken and Dumplings:** This hearty dish features tender chicken, fluffy dumplings, and a savory broth made with homemade chicken stock and canned vegetables such as carrots, corn, and green beans.

- **Strawberry Preserves Thumbprint Cookies:** These cookies are a delightful way to enjoy the sweetness of strawberry preserves. The cookie dough is rolled in sugar and then indented with a thumbprint, which is filled with strawberry preserves before baking. The result is a sweet and buttery cookie with a burst of fruity flavor.

- **Canned Peach Cobbler:** Peach cobbler is a classic dessert that is perfect for any occasion. This recipe uses canned peaches, along with a buttery biscuit topping, to create a warm and comforting dessert that will have everyone asking for seconds.

- **Sweet and Sour Meatballs**: These tender meatballs are coated in a tangy sauce made with canned pineapple, vinegar, and brown sugar. Serve them over rice for a quick and easy dinner.

- **Amish Ham and Bean Soup:** This flavorful soup is made with a combination of canned beans, ham, and vegetables such as celery, onions, and carrots. It's a hearty and comforting meal that's perfect for a cold winter day.

- **Canned Green Bean Casserole:** Green bean casserole is a staple of many holiday meals. This recipe uses canned green beans, along with a creamy mushroom sauce and crispy fried onions, to create a comforting and nostalgic dish that everyone will love.

- **Apple Butter Pork Chops**: This recipe uses apple butter, a delicious spread made from apples and spices, to create a sweet and savory glaze for pork chops. The result is a flavorful and tender pork chop that is perfect for any night of the week.

- **Old-Fashioned Bread and Butter Pickles:** These sweet and tangy pickles are made with cucumbers, onions, vinegar, and spices. They're the perfect accompaniment to a sandwich or burger.

- **Spiced Apple Rings:** These sweet and spicy apple rings are made with canned apple slices and a combination of cinnamon, cloves, and sugar. They're the perfect accompaniment to pork chops or roasted chicken.

- **Canned Salsa Chicken:** This recipe uses canned salsa, along with chicken breasts and a few other simple ingredients, to create a quick and easy weeknight dinner. The salsa adds a zesty and flavorful kick to the chicken, making it a crowd-pleaser for the whole family.

- **Canned Peach and Blackberry Crisp:** This recipe combines two of summer's best fruits - peaches and blackberries - into a delicious and easy dessert. The canned peaches and blackberries are topped with a buttery crumble topping and baked until golden brown and bubbling.

- **Canned Green Tomato Relish:** Green tomato relish is a tangy and flavorful condiment that is perfect for topping burgers, hot dogs, or sandwiches. This recipe uses canned green tomatoes, along with onions, peppers, and vinegar, to create a delicious and versatile relish that is easy to make and store.

- **Canned Apple Pie Filling:** This recipe uses canned apple pie filling, along with a homemade crust, to create a classic apple pie that is perfect for any occasion. The filling is made with tender apples, cinnamon, and sugar, and is the perfect balance of sweet and tart.

The key to making the most of your canned and preserved foods is to have a variety of recipes on hand that make use of these ingredients. These 15 recipes are just a few examples of the many delicious and creative ways you can use canned and preserved foods to create meals that celebrate the bounty of the harvest. So get in the kitchen, pull out your jars of preserves and cans of fruits and vegetables, and let your imagination run wild!

Tips for Making Homemade Baby Food

As you embark on the beautiful journey of motherhood, there is nothing quite as precious as nourishing your little one with homemade baby food. The Amish community has long known the importance of creating wholesome meals for their little ones, using their time-honored wisdom to craft recipes that are both nutritious and delicious.

Creating nourishing, homemade baby food is a wonderful way to ensure that your little one receives the best possible start in life. By making your own baby food, you have complete control over the ingredients, allowing you to create healthy and delicious meals that are tailored to your baby's needs. Here are some tips from the Amish community on making homemade baby food:

- **Choose Fresh, Organic Ingredients**: When making baby food, it is important to use fresh, organic ingredients that are free from pesticides and other harmful chemicals. The Amish take great care to grow their own fruits and vegetables, using traditional, sustainable farming practices to ensure that their produce is of the highest quality.

- **Cook the Food Thoroughly:** When preparing baby food, it is important to cook the food thoroughly to ensure that it is safe and easy for your baby to digest. The Amish often use traditional cooking methods, such as steaming or roasting, to ensure that the food is cooked through without losing its nutritional value.

- **Blend the Food to a Smooth Consistency:** For babies who are just starting to eat solid foods, it is important to blend the food to a smooth consistency to make it easy for them to swallow. The Amish use traditional food mills and blenders to create silky smooth purees that are perfect for babies.

- **Experiment with Different Flavors:** One of the joys of making homemade baby food is the ability to experiment with different flavors and textures. The Amish often use herbs and spices to add flavor to their baby food, introducing babies to a wide range of tastes and textures from an early age.

- **Store the Food Properly:** When storing homemade baby food, it is important to use airtight containers and to refrigerate or freeze the food to ensure that it stays fresh and safe for your baby to eat. The Amish use traditional canning and preserving techniques to store their baby food, ensuring that it stays fresh and nutritious for months to come.

- **If Possible, Involve Your Baby in the Process:** Making homemade baby food can be a wonderful bonding experience between you and your little one. The Amish often involve their babies in the cooking process, allowing them to smell and taste different ingredients, and introducing them to the joys of healthy eating from an early age.

Making homemade baby food is a wonderful way to ensure that your baby receives the best possible nutrition. By following these tips from the Amish community, you can create delicious and healthy meals that are tailored to your baby's needs, while also creating a deep connection between you and your little one through the joy of cooking.

Tips for Making Homemade Pet Food

Pets are more than just animals – they are beloved members of our families. As such, it is important to provide them with the best possible nutrition to ensure their health and happiness. Homemade pet food is a wonderful way to show your furry friends how much you care, while also ensuring that they are getting the highest quality ingredients and nutrients.

Here are some tips for making homemade pet food that will nourish your pets with love and care:

- **Consult with a Veterinarian:** Before making any changes to your pet's diet, it is important to consult with a veterinarian. They can advise you on your pet's nutritional needs and help you develop a balanced diet that meets their specific requirements.

- **Use High-Quality Ingredients:** Just like with human food, the quality of the ingredients you use in your pet's food will have a significant impact on their health. Look for high-quality meats, vegetables, and grains that are free from additives and preservatives.

- **Variety is Key:** Just like humans, pets benefit from a varied diet. Try incorporating different types of meat and vegetables into your pet's meals to provide a range of nutrients and flavors.

- **Cook Thoroughly:** It is important to cook homemade pet food thoroughly to eliminate any potential bacteria that could make your pet sick. Be sure to cook meat all the way through and avoid using raw eggs.

- **Consider Supplements:** Depending on your pet's needs, supplements such as omega-3 fatty acids and vitamins may be necessary to ensure they are getting all of the nutrients they need.

- **Store Properly:** Homemade pet food can be stored in the refrigerator or freezer, depending on the recipe. Be sure to store it in airtight containers and label them with the date to ensure freshness.

By following these tips, you can create homemade pet food that is both delicious and nutritious for your furry friends. So, roll up your sleeves, get in the kitchen, and start cooking up some love for your furry friends today!

Ideas for Gift-Giving with Canned and Preserved Foods

There is something special about giving and receiving homemade gifts, especially those that are made with love and care. Canned and preserved foods are a perfect gift for any occasion, as they not only taste delicious but also provide nourishment and comfort to those who receive them. In this section, we will explore some ideas for gift-giving with canned and preserved foods, from simple jars of jam to elaborate gift baskets.

Step 1: Choose the Right Recipe

The first step in creating a perfect gift with canned and preserved foods is to choose the right recipe. Consider the recipient's taste preferences, as well as the occasion for which you are making the gift. For example, a spicy jalapeno jelly might be a great gift for a friend who loves heat, while a classic strawberry jam would be perfect for a family member's breakfast table.

Step 2: Decorate the Jar

Once you have chosen the right recipe, it's time to decorate the jar. This is where you can get creative and add a personal touch to your gift. Tie a ribbon around the jar, attach a handwritten note, or add a custom label with the recipe name and ingredients. You can also add a decorative lid, such as a fabric square or a crocheted cover, to make the jar extra special.

Step 3: Create a Gift Basket

If you want to go the extra mile, consider creating a gift basket with multiple canned and preserved foods. Choose a theme, such as "breakfast essentials" or "picnic snacks," and include a variety of jars that complement each other. Add some fresh produce or homemade baked goods to complete the basket.

Step 4: Add a Personal Touch

Finally, don't forget to add a personal touch to your gift. Include a handwritten note or a card expressing your love and gratitude for the recipient. You can also share the story behind the recipe, or include a photo of you and the recipient enjoying a meal together.

Gift Ideas:

- A jar of homemade apple butter, tied with a red ribbon, makes a perfect gift for a neighbor or teacher.
- For a wedding or housewarming gift, create a basket with a variety of canned and preserved foods, such as pickles, salsa, and strawberry jam.
- A jar of spicy jalapeno jelly, decorated with a green ribbon, would be a great gift for a friend who loves to cook.
- For a holiday gift, create a basket with a variety of canned fruits and vegetables, such as applesauce, pumpkin puree, and pickled beets.
- A jar of homemade salsa, tied with a yellow ribbon, would be a great gift for a co-worker or boss.

In conclusion, canned and preserved foods make a wonderful and thoughtful gift for any occasion. By choosing the right recipe, decorating the jar, creating a gift basket, and adding a personal touch, you can create a gift that not only tastes great but also shows your love and care for the recipient. Spread love and nourishment with every jar!

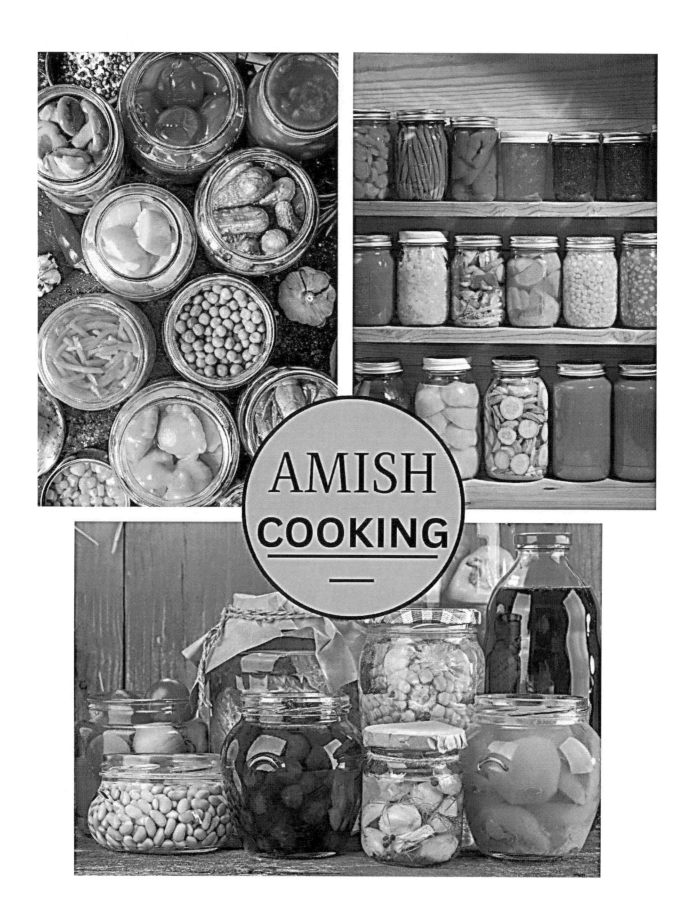

AMISH
COOKING

CONCLUSION

As we come to the end of this Amish canning and preserving cookbook, we hope that you have gained a deeper appreciation for the art and tradition of preserving food. Canning and preserving is more than just a way to preserve food for the winter months; it is a way of life that connects us to our past, our community, and our environment. It is a way to preserve the bounty of the harvest, and to share it with our loved ones and neighbors.

We have shared with you some of our most treasured recipes, techniques, and tips for canning and preserving a wide variety of foods. We hope that you have found them useful, and that you have been inspired to try them out in your own kitchen. We also hope that you have discovered the joy and satisfaction of making your own homemade jams, jellies, pickles, and more.

As you continue on your canning and preserving journey, we urge you to preserve not just the food, but also the traditions and values that go with it. Take the time to connect with your community, to share your knowledge and skills with others, and to pass on the tradition of canning and preserving to future generations. Preserve not just the food, but also the memories and stories that go with it. These are the things that will truly nourish us, and sustain us through the years.

And so, we leave you with a final recipe, one that has been passed down through generations of our family, and embodies the spirit of canning and preserving. It is a recipe for elderberry jam, made with wild elderberries that grow in abundance throughout the countryside. It is a simple recipe, but one that is filled with love, tradition, and the bounty of the earth.

ELDERBERRY JAM RECIPE

Ingredients:

- 4 cups elderberries, stems removed
- 3 cups sugar
- 1/4 cup lemon juice

Instructions:

- In a large pot, combine the elderberries, sugar, and lemon juice.
- Heat the mixture over medium heat, stirring occasionally, until the sugar has dissolved.
- Bring the mixture to a boil, then reduce the heat and let it simmer for 20-30 minutes, stirring occasionally, until the mixture thickens and reaches the desired consistency.
- Ladle the hot jam into sterilized jars, leaving 1/4 inch of headspace.
- Process the jars in a boiling water bath for 10 minutes.
- Remove the jars from the water bath and let them cool completely before storing them in a cool, dark place.

We hope that this elderberry jam recipe, and all of the other recipes in this cookbook, will bring you joy, nourishment, and a deeper connection to the land and community around you.

As this cookbook comes to an end, we want to express our gratitude to each and every one of you who have joined us on this journey. We hope that this book will serve as a reminder of the power of community, the beauty of nature, and the importance of preserving traditions for future generations.

Eli and I wish you many happy years of canning and preserving ahead. Cheers!

FOR ANY QUESTIONS OR FURTHER ASSITANCE WITH REGARDS TO THE RECIPES IN THIS BOOK, CONTACT ME VIA EMAIL: iamgeorginatracy7@gmail.com. **WE WILL BE GLAD TO ASSIST YOU.**

Made in United States
Orlando, FL
20 May 2025

61433836R10070